GOODNIGHT SWEETHEART

Life and Times of Al Bowlly

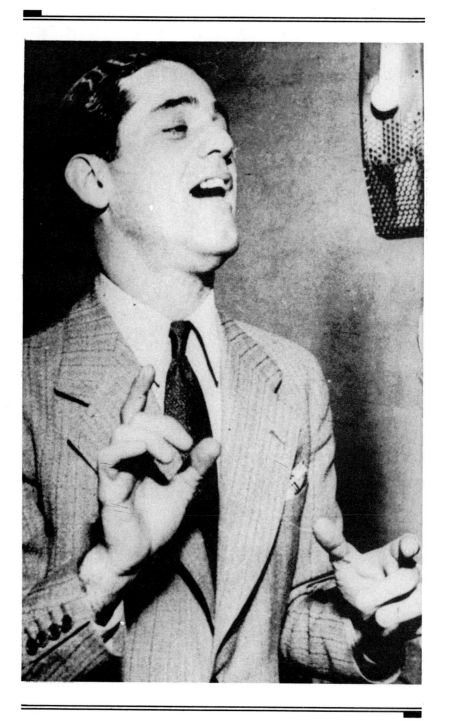

GOODNIGHT SWEETHEART
Life and Times of Al Bowlly

by
Ray Pallett

SPELLMOUNT LTD
Tunbridge Wells, Kent

*This book is dedicated to my late father, Reginald Pallett
who had a great knowledge of and enthusiasm for
Al Bowlly and the music of the 1930s.*

In the same *Recollections* series
Don't Fuss, Mr Ambrose
Memoirs of a life spent in Popular Music by Billy Amstell.

First published in UK in 1986 by
SPELLMOUNT LTD
12 Dene Way, Speldhurst,
Tunbridge Wells, Kent TN3 0NX
ISBN: 0–946771–60–X (UK)

British Library Cataloguing in Publication Data
Pallett, Ray
  Goodnight sweetheart: the life & times of
  Al Bowlly. — (Recollections)
  1. Bowlly, Al   2. Singers — Biography
  I. Title   II. Series
  784'.092'4   ML420.B/

Design by Words & Images, Speldhurst, Tunbridge Wells, Kent
Typeset by Metra Graphic, Tunbridge Wells, Kent
Printed by Staples Printers Rochester Limited, Love Lane, Rochester, Kent

Contents

Acknowledgements

Al Bowlly was a very private person who gave very little away about himself. The result is that there were virtually no sources of information that were both detailed and accurate. The information in this book came from countless sources, most providing only fragments – each just one piece of a jigsaw puzzle. It would be impractical to list all these sources here. However, I would like to record my thanks in public to the following people who have contributed more substantially to the production of this book.

Edgar Adeler, Horst Bergmeier, Mish Bowlly, Roger Bugg MA, Bert Davenport, John Edwardes, Vince Egan, Chris Ellis, Jack Forehan, Roy Fox, Joe Gold, Chris Hayes, Mrs Doris James, Mitri Kourie, Sydney Lipton, Gerry Moore, Bill Moreton, Alfred Ne-Jame, Ray Noble, Bill Outlaw, Mrs Lew Stone, H. J. Strachan, Paul Turnell, Frank Wappat, Bert Wilcox and Graham Webb.

I would also like to mention my wife, Jeanette, who has been so helpful throughout the production of this book.

Much information and most of the photographs have come from the files of *Memory Lane*. This magazine specialises in dance music and jazz of the 1920s, 1930s and 1940s and is published from 40 Merryfield Approach, Leigh-on-Sea, Essex, SS9 4HJ, England.

CHAPTER ONE

Who Am I?

All over the world there is a nostalgia boom; there is little doubt about it. Films, radio, television, records, books and even clothes are all harking back to the past. Not only old and middle-aged folk are looking back – but the young are as well.

And when it comes to British singers and dance music of the pre-war days the biggest name all over the world is AL BOWLLY. During most of the 1930s Al was Britain's leading popular singer and was known as Britain's 'Ambassador of Song'.

Although he is now Britain's biggest name in nostalgia, in his heyday during the 1930s, Al never won the fame he deserved. It is even said that he is more famous today than he was then, although he is now definitely recognised as Britain's leading light in that era of popular song. Even though the competition was good, Al was a head and shoulders above his nearest rivals when it came to his artistry and originality, but his popularity rating did not always reflect this.

Pop music, or dance music as it was then called, did not have the huge following and the publicity machinery that it has today, but, because of the many beautiful songs written in that decade, that period has become known as the golden era of music and song. Al Bowlly was a part of that era, he was called the 'singing nomad', because of his extensive travels around the world.

In the 1920s, 'the jazz age', the music of the moment was jazz orientated dance music such as the *Charleston* and *Black Bottom*. Vocal-wise, the 'Jolsonish' style of singing was in vogue. Later, the dance music became sweeter and more sophisticated and the shouting style vocals gave way to 'crooning'. During the 1930s, the listening public decidely liked its music sweet and so the majority of dance records sold were waltzes and foxtrots. Subsequently, the American big band sound became in vogue and soon many English bands were playing in that style. During the 1920s and 1930s the dance band was the main attraction in the field of popular music but at the outbreak of war the vocalists were becoming the main attraction and soon were to overtake the dance bands in popularity, thus bringing the dance band era to a close.

Al Bowlly recorded with all manner of dance bands ranging from big progressive units, such as those led by Ray Noble and Geraldo to small and obscure instrumental groups. Most of Al's records were made as a band singer although he did make numerous recordings as a soloist. The term 'solo' used throughout this book is to distinguish between the records he made as featured vocalist with a dance band and those on which he was the principal artiste. On those latter solo records Al is usually accompanied by a small orchestra or piano and guitar. Although other crooners were crooning in London before Al, it was he who first became a solo variety act, became the first popular singer to get a solo spot on the BBC and who was the first British popular singer to be invited to work in America. Bowlly was Britain's first *pop singer*, the first man in this country to become a true 'song stylist' – using the microphone and amplification to project his own personality. During the 1930s the popular music world in Britain was very different from what it was in America or what it is in this country today. One of the main differences was America's commercial radio, just made for entertainers such as Bing Crosby, and the other was their film industry. No one ever highlighted or publicised British popular singers.

Comparing the scene of pre-war Britain to that of today, the exploits of our singers are frequently headline if not front page news in the popular press. However, when he left for America in 1934, there was just a small piece inside the *Daily Herald* saying that bandleader Ray Noble was going to the States and taking with him singer Al Bowlly. And, incidentally, when he arrived in America he certainly noticed the enormous difference between the New York and London music scene.

Radio listeners in Great Britain did not only listen to BBC programmes, but also continental stations, the most popular being Radio Luxembourg and Radio Normandy, which beamed programmes of popular appeal to Britain. The success of these overseas commercial stations was due to the fact that the BBC failed on many occasions to give the British people what they wanted to listen to. At one stage they even banned the singing of song words on the air as it was considered that the song publishers were getting a free advertisement for their numbers. During his career Al Bowlly made both solo appearances and sung with various bands on British, Continental and American radio.

True, there are thousands of people who look back and listen with a nostalgic fondness, but there are also many who were born after Al's death that are just as enthusiastic. To these people, it is not nostalgia. When they hear for the first time another 'Bowlly' vocal, it is equivalent to a pop fan initially hearing the latest record of his favourite idol.

You may ask 'Why Al Bowlly?' Why a book about a man who was essentially a band singer and as such was one amongst hundreds? Al appears on just over 600 78 rpm records from the period 1927–41. Surely it takes more than 600 scratchy records to justify a book on a singer?

Yes, there is something special about the singer Al Bowlly. About the voice. About the man. Something that keeps thousands of his original fans interested and captures the imagination of new followers every day. Even though it is over 45 years since he died, the voice and personality are still with us. It has been said that when Al sings, it is as if he sings to *you*, personally, even if it is over the radio or a gramophone record. His voice and artistry live on through all these years of change and progress. Further interest has been aroused due to mystery surrounding the singer. In his heyday no one really knew what nationality his parents were or how old he was. These facts and others have only come to light during research in recent years. Myths, half-truths and stories have been woven into a tangle of romantic fiction concerning this small, dusky society favourite of the 1930s.

The answer to the question 'Why Al Bowlly?' is not just that he had a unique voice. Combine this with legends and Bowlly's vibrant personality which has remained something of an enigma, and you may begin to have the answer. It could have been Sam Browne or Chick Henderson, two other singers from the Bowlly era who actually beat Al in popularity; but these two have almost drifted into obscurity.

The voice of Al Bowlly has a remarkable range, greater than many of his contemporaries or successors, and seems as if Al could sing baritone, tenor, alto and fallsetto, although he was generally billed as a baritone. Although he

was considered a *crooner*, this word does not do justice to Al's voice. Bowlly himself disliked it, preferring to call his art 'singing in the modern microphone manner'. Despite the large number of records made by Al, people who heard him sing live have said that no gramophone record can capture the true Bowlly charisma. There were better singers around but Al's voice was unique. He did not copy anyone's style and no one really set out to copy his. Some have commented that on occasions Al copied Bing Crosby, but this is not true taken in isolation as both singers had their own style. Bing originated a style of singing that set the standard for the 1930s, and because of this one could argue that every popular singer of the period was influenced by Bing. Some made every effort to sound like him. One band vocalist, Denny Dennis, was often billed as 'England's Bing Crosby', while Al Bowlly was referred to as 'England's answer to Bing Crosby' which, of course, is a completely different statement.

His full range can be heard on such numbers as *If You'll Say 'Yes'*, *Cherie*, *Love is the Sweetest Thing* and *Blue Moon*. He had a strong sense of rhythm and a feel for music and these qualities came over in his singing. Al's vibrato and intonation were perfect and his diction good, although at times there is a trace of Cockney accent. He did, in fact, use a dictionary to help get pronunciation correct! Al could sing in several foreign languages including Afrikaans and Yiddish.

Al could sing all sorts of numbers including jazz, blues, comedy, country and ballads. Examples are *You Ought to See Sally on a Sunday* (jazz); *Twentieth Century Blues* (blues); *Little Nell* (comedy); and *Louisiana Hayride* (country). As regards balladeering, it was as a singer of romantic ballads that Al really excelled and won his reputation. A good selection of such songs would be some of the Ray Noble compositions including *By the Fireside*, *The Very Thought of You* and *The Touch of Your Lips*.

By listening to these it should be evident that Al Bowlly was able to get right into a song and enact its meaning; no other singer then or since has put so much into a song as Al did. It is interesting to quote Bowlly's own words upon this aspect of popular singing:

'If you cannot impress yourself with the story you are conveying through the medium of your voice, how can you expect to impress others? If it is a sad lyric it is not sufficient for you to be sad – you must be moved. If your lyric expresses grief, you must live for a moment in the atmosphere of the story and be grief-stricken. A lot depends on your sensitivity to the emotions. If you can feel to the fullest degree anger, pain, fear, love, hate, sorrow and happiness, they will animate your song and give it an artistic value. Without these emotions your voice is worthless whether it has quality or not.'

This is borne out by bandleader Ray Noble who remembers that having sung a song with a poignant lyric, Bowlly had turned away from the

10

Before we conclude this consideration of the voice of Al Bowlly, let us take a quote from Maurice Elwyn, a contemporary of Al's, from the magazine *Rhythm* of October 1934:

'There are two classes of "crooner". One is the stylist and the other is what I may call the "honest-to-goodness" type. Al Bowlly is essentially in the former class, sometimes even sacrificing quality for the sake of style. As this pleases his many admirers, one can hardly blame him for adopting this course, although it may not fit in with the true art of singing.

But do not run away with the idea that Al Bowlly is just a "crooner". As a teacher of legitimate singing myself, let me inform you that he is one of the most natural singers we have. I would describe his voice as "foreign" in quality and one that never really gets a chance to show what it can do.

I have heard Al singing at a time when he thought nobody was listening to him. This came about because he lives in the block of flats adjacent to mine. You can take it from me that, when he wants to, Al Bowlly can get some real delivery behind his notes and can just as easily emerge from his restraint as a pukka serenader, without the need of a microphone to amplify his voice.

To the people who have imagined that Al Bowlly has suffered from a severe attack of "Bing Crosby" fever, let me once and for all assure them that, long before Crosby was known, our Al was using – in a modified way – the same delightful style and tricks that he now employs in his work.

He sings in the most natural manner and makes it quite apparent to both listener and observer that singing to him is as natural as eating and drinking – and just as necessary. Al has, of course, many "tricks" which he uses with remarkable effect. But I do not recommend vocalists to copy him to the extent of trying to imitate his particular quality. This would undoubtedly lead to sore throats and hoarseness. Al Bowlly's "tricks" are part of his own natural artistry – they are for Al Bowlly and nobody else.'

Although I believe Al Bowlly to be as good a singer as the foregoing paragraphs suggest, I should stress that he was never a famous personality. Star singers of popular songs just did not exist then in this country. Having looked at the voice and singing style, which undoubtedly accounts for much of the interest in Al Bowlly, the next factor to be considered is the Bowlly personality, which will unfold in greater detail during the course of this book.

Al always created a good impression with whoever he met, and like his idol, Bing Crosby, was and is admired by both men and women. He was admired by, and popular with, not only his audience, but show-business folk as well. He could well be described as 'the artiste's artiste'.

Al Bowlly had a wide range of admirers in the business ranging from the late radio and television personality Gilbert Harding, to 1950s singer Dickie

Valentine (who once said he learnt a lot from listening to fellow South African Bowlly) and actor and broadcaster Hubert Gregg. Gregg, who presents some nostalgic radio programmes for the BBC, said in an interview that his favourite period in entertainment was the 1930s and if forced to choose any particular artiste as his favourite, it would be Al Bowlly.

As a dance band singer, he was one among many, but if Al was singing on the stage, there was a certain *presence*. As a professional, Al was always very anxious to please whoever he was working for.

As a person, Al Bowlly was unaffected and natural, he usually had a bright optimism, was emotional and fastidious. 'Al was in the depths of depression one moment and on top of the world the next!' These sentiments have been echoed by those who knew Al, but it is not that easy to weigh up a man's personality. Chris Hayes of *Melody Maker* says that Al was quiet, modest and introvert, although he was gifted with great personal charm and was a bit of a raconteur. A friend who knew Al quite well told me that if you ever met him in the street, he would greet you as if you were the one person in the world that he wanted to see. It was natural for Al to greet somebody that way whoever they were. Even if he had had a blazing row with someone the day before, he bore no malice.

Al was a happy-go-lucky sort of chap whose philosophy was *live for the day* and he can be quoted as saying 'Life is great. But always remember one thing. When you awake to a new day, live for that day.'

He was a born gambler and sportsman. He was keen on physical culture – after his voice, this was his passion in life. He was tough and a fighter.

Often, during press interviews, Al would embellish the truth. It is this fact that has accounted for most of the fables and folk-lore that have surrounded Al. Being a 'story teller' what Al told the press and what was printed in the articles contained much fiction. Here are a few examples:

Al told Lew Stone that he was born in 1890 for the purpose of an official form. Yet he recorded 1898 for all other purposes. He told at least two completely different stories as to how he got his first professional job with bandleader Edgar Adeler, neither of which were true. And the story of how he auditioned for Roy Fox differs when told by Fox and Bowlly.

Al just made up and romanticised incidents to make his story more interesting. How was he to know that about 50 years later anyone would be interested in his life? More people seem interested in his life now than then. And this leads on to what is probably the biggest myth of all – the degree of fame and popularity attributed to him.

The fact is that Al was not a 'star'. His name was not a household word. In recent years, much has been written about Al and in far too many instances he has been referred to as a 'star' or a 'famous man'. 'He was almost as big as Bing Crosby.' 'He was immensely popular both in the UK and the USA as a result of personal appearances there and all over the world as a result of his many records.' 'Al Bowlly became a star on the crest of this wave.'

'The entire Roy Fox band broadcasts were centered around Al.' The foregoing statements have all been written about him over the years and typify the exaggeration of his popularity. I have quizzed many people as to how big Al was and have received answers ranging from 'Any man in the street would know him' to 'Unknown to anyone who did not "follow" dance band vocalists'. However, the more discerning sources confirm that Al was not famous, a view endorsed by journalists and musicians around at the time.

Al worked in America in the mid-1930s and several people who were connected with him have said in interviews that America was not the success for Al that it should have been. However, most articles about Al in the USA state that he was very popular there, even beating Crosby in the popularity stakes. Ray Noble has stated that in the USA, Al received 'wild' fan mail and that he left a trail of broken female hearts behind him. The fact is that he became a very successful band singer in America, but never achieved individual stardom like the famous bandleaders.

In conclusion, I believe the truth of the matter is that to anyone who had an interest in dance music, the name 'Bowlly' was a fairly important one. But to others, the name would mean very little.

Having briefly looked at the man, the voice and the legend, I hope I have aroused your interest sufficiently for you to read the rest of the book. Each chapter looks at an era of Al's life and has, as its title that of an appropriate song that was recorded by him.

As you read this book, whether you will be taking a stroll down memory lane, or were born after it all happened, you will be reading about one of the most fascinating personalities in popular music's history.

CHAPTER TWO

Song of the Wanderer
1899–1920

Al Bowlly was christened Albert Alick Bowlly and was born in Maputo, Mozambique on 7 January 1899. His birth was registered retrospectively on 19 February 1903 at Durban after the family had moved to South Africa. However, the birth certificate remained untraced until 1983.

There has, in fact, always been controversy over the date of Al's birth. He himself always maintained that he was born in 1898. Even the age stated on the certificate of his first marriage and his death certificate indicate that he was born in 1898 – but these documents are no proof of a man's age. Added to this, it was firmly believed by many that 1890 was nearer his true year of birth. To add weight to this view, in the *Melody Maker* of 25 April 1941, the columnist who wrote Al's epitaph said that he was older than anyone thought. Lew Stone, with whom Al worked for many years, once said that Al admitted to being 42 in 1932 for the purpose of the completion of an 'official' form. And in 1938, in a conversation with a friend, Al claimed he was then 46. In more recent years, surviving members of the Lew Stone Band have referred to Al as the 'Daddy of the Band'. It seems quite possible that Al did not know his true date of birth.

The Bowlly family believed Al was born in 1900 as indicated below in an extract of a letter I received prior to the tracing of the birth certificate. It was thoroughly researched and came from Al's nephew, Mr Mitri Kourie in 1976 containing the birthdates of Al's brothers and sisters; all the dates have been verified by the surviving brothers and sisters and their children.

The extract is reproduced below. (The square brackets indicate the author's insertions.)

Theodora born 11 June 1894. (She always boasted that she was the same age as the Prince of Wales.) [later King Edward VIII].
Matthew born 15 January 1896.
Augustus born 23 July 1898.
Albert born 7 January 1900. (My mother is quite adamant about this, and knowing her character, I am convinced this is the correct date.)
Emily born 12 May 1901. [Emily celebrated her 79th birthday in 1980.]

16

Harriet	born 17 July 1905. (Between Emily and Harriet was born George who died a child of 11 years.)
Rose	born 11 January 1908. (My mother.)
Michael	born 19 September 1910 – known as Mish.
Julia	born 4 September 1911.
Leonora	born 11 May 1917.

Returning to Al's family origins, which are rather obscure, his father, Alick Pauli was Greek by nationality, being born on the island of Rhodes in 1867. By religion he was Greek Orthodox. Al's mother, born Miriam Ayoub-NeeJame in 1874, was Lebanese and of the Catholic religion. They first met in Australia where Miriam's brother, who had previously worked in Egypt, had emigrated and spent months at a time trading in the outback. When he had established himself in Australia, he sent for his sister. However when she arrived in Australia her brother was away in the outback and returned very angry to find that one of the family had 'married off' his sister at a very young age to a Lebanese–Greek by the name of Pauli. The marriage took place on 6 April 1892 in the Catholic Cathedral at Perth and the certificate reads *Alick Pauli, son of Dimetri: Miriam Ayoub, daughter of Azad Ayoub*. Both were described as 'hawkers'. Soon after the marriage the newly-weds went to Africa.

There has also been much discussion as to how the name *Bowlly* came about: it does not seem like a Greek name. Apparently, Al's father's Greek surname was virtually unpronounceable in English, a language that he could neither read or write. His two forenames were Alexis Paulos. Mish Bowlly and his sister Nora think that their father when in Beirut in the early 1890s changed 'Paulos' to 'Pauli' as it was more English sounding. Al's father who spoke thickly, pronounced 'Ps' like 'Bs' and when his passport was made out, the name 'Pauli' was erroneously entered by the clerk as 'Bowlly' (the original unpronounceable surname being dropped altogether.) From there on 'he was stuck with it', according to Mish and by the time Miriam and Alick had reached Africa, their name had become 'Bowlly'.

When the Bowllys arrived in Africa they landed at Lourenco Marques, (now Maputo) in Portuguese East Africa (now Mozambique), where Al was born. He was still very young when the family moved to South Africa, first stopping briefly at Durban, then on to Pietermaritzburg and it was here that Al's parents were naturalised on 21 February 1903. From there they went to Johannesburg where Al was brought up and where, after 80 years, Al's younger brother Mish still resides.

In Jo'burg the Bowlly family moved to No 10 Pritchard Street which was in the centre of the town and next to the Star Newspaper building. Alick Bowlly soon established himself in business buying and selling jewellery and as a contrast, also sold fruit and vegetables in the Newtown Market. In the United Transvaal Directory (a business directory) he was described as a 'General Dealer'.

Up to around 1910 there was no Greek Orthodox Church in Jo'burg, so all the Bowlly children, other than the last three were baptised by the Catholic Church. Al was later baptised by the Greek Orthodox Church which faith he kept throughout his life.

Al's nickname in the family was 'Bootie', Afrikaans for brother, but was often called 'Portjie' (pronounced 'Pour-kee' and derived from words meaning 'Little Portuguese'). All of his early life was spent in Jo'burg, where he attended Newtown school, and, although he got good school reports, especially in music and scripture, he was a truant, describing himself in later life as a 'ruffian'. When Al spoke to the press in a 1938 interview, he told of how he fell in love with his teacher, Miss McGill, when he was 14. This is probably no more than Al's romantic fiction. However, the Transvaal Education Department confirm Bertha McGill was teaching at Newtown School from 25 March 1913 until 1 April 1914 and in possession of the author is a book discovered by Mish entitled *Across Two Seas* by H. A. Forbes and inscribed 'Awarded to Albert Bowlly, June 1913 from B. McGill'. (This inscription, incidentally, has been verified as authentic by the British Museum.) All through his school days Al proved himself to be good at sport and he maintained his interest in it throughout his life. At his school there were good music and singing teachers and he was a very eager pupil. He sang in a local choir, where he was taught still more about singing and music.

School hours were from 9am – 3.30pm and at the age of nine, realising that he had time on his hands and that he could contribute to the family budget, his parents arranged for him to help out in a nearby barbershop, run by his Greek uncle Christos, where he would sweep the floor and occasionally lather a customer.

When he was 14 he left school to work full time in the barbershop where he was taught the hairdressing trade as were his brothers Mish and Gus. In 1933, at the age of 21, Perry Como who achieved fame as a singer in the post-war era, had established himself as a barber in his home town, but about 15 years previously in South Africa, Al Bowlly, by the end of his teens, was running his own barbershop located in Jo'burg's Nugget Street. Al later told the press that this shop was a present from his father, which is confirmed by his brother Mish but adds that the shop didn't last long because Al was not really interested in hairdressing – he wanted to become a full time entertainer. He was music mad, playing banjo, ukelele and singing and he got his inspiration from the African mine boys. In the evenings he would sometimes do a gig for which he is reputed to have earned ten shillings a time. Al became known as the 'Singing Barber' and by this time he had left the parental home to live in a flat by himself.

Not only did Al do evening work as a singer and musician, he did, according to brother Mish, also do a variety act. In this he would impersonate Charlie Chaplin for which he won a silver cup, still in the possession of Mish.

Al's first break into the entertainment world came in the early 1920s

Al's impression of Charlie Chaplin

Edgar Adeler, with whom Al obtained his first full-time professional singing job

when he was given a part-time job with a local musical group as vocalist doubling on ukelele, and played at the newly-opened Tattersall Club in Kerk Street on Saturday nights. Al managed to get this job because one of his brothers knew the group's violinist, Julius Miller. The other member of the group was a pianist from London, Harry Saville.

Al must now have had ambitions to travel outside South Africa as in 1921 he made his passport application. He also applied to become a naturalised South African, his Certificate of Naturalisation being dated 12 March 1921. This also made him British something of which he was very proud, becoming a very patriotic Briton.

What is also virtually unknown is that Al formally learnt to play the concertina, ukelele and banjo around this time and that he also received singing lessons from Letty Campbell, a professional vocalist and pianist in Jo'burg. This is contrary to the old myth that Al 'never had a singing lesson in his life'.

Meanwhile, the principal dance band organisation in Jo'burg, Clark and Adeler, were riding high. They controlled around ten bands and were the official suppliers of popular music for four Governor General's functions at Government House in Pretoria. When he heard of the band at the new dance club, Edgar Adeler admits that the news had him worrying since he had never experienced any real opposition. However, the opposition did not last long because dissension arose, resulting in Al Bowlly offering his services to Adeler.

Edgar Adeler recalls that Al was in his opinion definitely the king pin of the act and that he made Al an attractive offer. Adeler considered him a big asset in the Clark and Adeler empire, having a fine personality and a voice 'out of this world'. Now that Al had signed with Clark and Adeler, his professional career had really started. This was to be a big adventure which was to take him high and take him low and on which he was destined to sing his way around the world. His ambition was to sing in Europe and particularly in Britain and he little realised that one day he would land a top job in America, the traditional home of popular music.

There was, for a long time, much controversy as to how Al got his first job with Edgar Adeler. This was a most interesting contradiction because Al himself told two completely different versions.

In 1938, Al's life story was told in the magazine *Radio Pictorial* under the title 'My Life of Song'. In this Bowlly states that Edgar Adeler came to Jo'burg in 1923 and that Al went to listen to his band six nights running. On the sixth night Al plucked up the courage to ask Adeler for a job. Adeler offered him a job as guitarist but not vocalist. But, when Al was interviewed for an article in *Popular Song* in 1935 he stated that Adeler was a customer in his barber shop and while being shaved by an assistant, he overheard Al singing to himself at the back of the shop and offered him £10 a week to join his organisation.

It was not until contact had been made with two very helpful people in South Africa, jazz researcher Horst Bergmeier and Edgar Adeler himself that these two persistent myths, started by Bowlly himself, were laid to rest. Messrs Adeler and Bergmeier are in the main responsible for the information contained in the next two chapters.

CHAPTER THREE

Sunny Days
1922–25

Soon after Al had joined up with the Clark and Adeler organisation in 1922, Jimmy Clark received an offer to go to London and got Adeler to buy him out.

Jimmy Clark's departure coincided with an offer for Edgar Adeler to take his No 1 band to the Corner Lounge Tea Rooms which was a high class restaurant in Jo'burg's Pritchard Street and one of the few places in town able to employ a regular band. The offer came from restauranteur Mrs Sheffield and was for the band to play during the afternoons and Monday, Tuesday and Wednesday evenings. This proposal was particularly suitable as it did not interfere with Friday and Saturday nights which were the main times that the band were engaged elsewhere. Edgar Adeler recalls that he was then able to pay his musicians a guaranteed minimum of £10 a week, a figure unheard of for those days.

For the Corner House engagement, the group was re-named 'Edgar Adeler's Hawaiian Band' which was the type of music the audience expected to hear. Incidentally, they played opposite a classical trio led by Ernie Kapinski, a violinist from London who later became Bert Ambrose's favourite violinist under the name of Ernie Lewis.

Edgar Adeler's Hawaiian Band comprised: Johnny Jacobs (violin); Len Fillis (banjo and guitar); Al Bowlly (vocal and ukelele); Desmond Gregg (percussion and alto saxophone) and Edgar Adeler (leader and piano). Adeler recalls that Al Bowlly was the king pin of the band – 'practically indispensable'. One of the members of the group was to help Al Bowlly several years later when he eventually got to England. This was Len Fillis, who became one of England's leading guitarists around 1930 and who gave Al recording work when he had no regular job.

Edgar Adeler was now at the peak of his career. Considering the poor economy and that only two or three places in this comparatively small community and probably not more than five in the whole of South Africa could afford a regular band, Edgar was beginning to worry about maintaining his success. He probably also felt ready to spread his wings and try his luck overseas.

So Edgar approached the members of the band with a proposition. He suggested that they should leave South Africa and do a six-month trip around the East Coast through the Suez Canal and on to England where they could listen to the latest bands and safeguard against becoming stale. This may have been Adeler's idea, but the tour that lay ahead was very different. The plan was to work their way along the route to pay all expenses and that any profits were to be shared out among all.

Adeler put up £60 in advance advertising and paid the band's fares to Bulawayo, in Rhodesia where he had already received an offer to perform for one week.

Bill 'Swaddy' Swadling on trombone and 'Blackie' Blackwell, a runaway from the British army, on trumpet, were added to the band before they departed. Also included in the group were Edgar's wife and his father, a very experienced and successful manager in the entertainment business and invaluable for he had toured Rhodesia many times before and had all the right contacts.

After a farewell dance at the Selborne Hall which was a sellout, the seven-piece band set off from Jo'burg in July 1923, playing one night stands at Mafeking and Francistown en route to Bulawayo where they stayed for three days. Financially the band were doing very well, taking £50 in Mafeking and £25 in Francistown. Although they had been South Africa's top band, they were inexperienced in stage craft. Nevertheless, they improved as the tour continued. They played through several villages that were built around a pub, introducing the latest hit *Yes We Have No Bananas* and Adeler's own composition *Karoo*. Adeler believes his was the first band in Africa to play *Bananas*, which used to be a feature for Al.

Edgar recalls an incident that occurred at one of the villages in Rhodesia, Marrandellas:

> 'En route through Rhodesia we played at a one-eyed dorp (village) called Marrandellas. In those days it comprised of a small hotel and a few houses. Opposite the hotel frontage was bare veld. After our arrival and settling in to our various rooms, Desmond Gregg, my drummer, beckoned to me to come to his room which he shared with Al, who was eslewhere meeting some bods. He pointed to Al's suitcase, lying open on his bed. There on top was a knuckle-duster. I'd never seen one before, and haven't seen one since. But one glance and I knew what it was. Disgustedly I just took hold of it, walked on to the verandah in front of us and threw it far into the veld. I never heard a word from Al that it was missing.'

At this time Len Fillis decided to quit the band and return to Port Elizabeth to marry his fiancée, and Al Bowlly was to benefit from Len's defection. Edgar Adeler got Bowlly to learn the tenor banjo. Adeler recalls that he had some private engagements as a solo pianist and that he wanted Bowlly to accompany him on the banjo as well, of course, as singing. Bowlly mastered the banjo and was able to take over at a moment's notice when Len Fillis made his exit.

The band continued to tour Rhodesia and visited Broken Hill and Salisbury where they had shows booked at the City Hall for one week. When they had reached Salisbury, Adeler received a cable from Edgar Warwick offering the band a year's contract to tour the Far East. Without hesitation, Adeler and the boys accepted this offer and the original plans to travel to England were shelved.

Presently, violinist Johnny Jacobs was to return to Jo'burg to take over the running of Adeler's band there, later to be replaced by Ernie Lewis from London although Adeler knew him from the Corner Lounge Tea Rooms.

With the tour of the Far East clinched, Adeler decided in the meantime to tour East Africa. From Salisbury they left for Beira in the then Portuguese East Africa (where Johnny Jacobs left), then on to Dar es Salaam and finally to Mombasa where they were promptly met by Ernie Lewis. The weeks until the boat for India arrived were spent in Nairobi with an engagement at the Royal Theatre and a score of private functions. By this time the group had become a much more polished act.

As regards Al Bowlly, Edgar Adeler says he was idolised in East Africa, and he recalls an incident where a wealthy lady fell madly in love with him and Edgar had to use a lot of tact to overcome the delicate situation!

The weeks quickly passed by and the boat arrived to take Adeler, Bowlly and the others to Bombay to start their tour of the Far East. Obviously, the band had gained a good reputation because, until they reached Bombay, Edgar Warwick, who brought them out, had not even heard them play.

Before the India tour was to commence, Edgar Warwick suggested that the name of the band be changed to add 'snob appeal' to The London Syncopating Orchestra.

India proved to be a great money spinner for this little outfit and from around November 1923 the band zig-zagged through India, playing at every conceivable place: one week at the Excelsior Theatre in Bombay followed by two weeks at the Empire in Calcutta. For one week they participated in the New Year's celebrations in the Calcutta Gardens followed by another spectacular festival in Allahabad. They spent three days with the 16th Lancers at Lucknow and played at the Delhi Club in Delhi and travelled through the Khyber Pass for a brief engagement at Landi Kotal, a forlorn outpost of the then British Empire. Agra and Hyderabad followed and the last performance given in India was at Madras.

From Madras they sailed for Penang in Malaya and worked their way south, playing at a one night stand at the famous Raffles Hotel in Singapore along the route. The popular belief that they played a residency at Raffles is definitely unfounded, according to Edgar Adeler and Desmond Gregg who were interviewed on the subject.

It was during this period that friction first started between Al Bowlly and

Edgar Adeler. This was often concerned with discipline etc and resulted in arguments between Bowlly, Adeler's father and Warwick. Edgar Adeler takes up the story of one particular incident which stuck in his mind and happened at Ipoh:

'It was all very trivial, but sad to say, very upsetting. It was a recognised feature of life in those parts to enjoy an afternoon siesta. We were booked in at a double storey Rest House, my Dad and I occupying a room on the first floor. We were in deep slumber when we were suddenly disturbed by Al bellowing loudly at a laundryman who obviously had displeased him with his washing chores. His voice of indignation penetrated throughout the Rest House waking us up. I laid there quietly while my Dad shouted out to Al to "SHUT UP". He yelled back "Shut up yourself, you old bastard". Now I was right in the middle. Al was the king pin of the show, practically indispensable. I could ill afford an argument with him thousands of miles away from home. So I kept a stiff upper lip, swallowed my pride, and pretended I was asleep, thought it rankled deeply in my heart. I just had to lie low and pretend I had heard nothing. It passed off on the surface but it lay latent in my sub-conscious mind.'

This and the other incidents blew over and after a very successful tour of the Malay States, the band set sail for Java. At Java, they opened at the Harmony Club in Jakarta, followed by an engagement at the British Club in Semarang. A large number of club dates followed together with a whole host of private engagements.

However, during this tour the final crunch came which resulted in Edgar Adeler dismissing Al Bowlly. Again, Adeler takes up the story:

'One night we were showing at some venue and everyone was in a good mood especially Al Bowlly. My spot of solo was in the second half and I was doing my stuff when suddenly Al threw a cushion at me in full view of the audience. Under ordinary circumstances I would have passed it off with a smile and a jest, but a flashback of the incident in the Malay States and I came off the stage fuming and lashed out at Al. He was of smaller stature than me but on the other hand I was no fighter or boxer and it developed into a brawl with both of us kind of wrestling on the floor until someone separated us. But I wasn't appeased and told him with a venomous tongue "You're fired." Our train left at 6am next morning. I was, at least, I thought I was, first to arrive at the station, but lo and behold, there was Al already comfortably seated in the reserved compartment. I went up to him and brusquely demanded him to get off the train, he was no longer a member of my group. He sheepishly left the compartment and we steamed out of the station sans Bowlly. It was such a drastic thing to do, but I've always had a streak of obstinacy in my make-up and I just wouldn't soften.'

Written on the reverse of the original photo 'Albert taken in my car – doesn't he look nice'

Despite the fact that Edgar Adeler considered Al Bowlly the king pin of the band he had now finally sacked him. It was September 1924; Al Bowlly's chair in the Adeler outfit was taken over by Eugene Pingatore, brother of Mike, Paul Whiteman's banjoist.

During his stay with Edgar Adeler, Al Bowlly was featured vocalist as well as playing the ukelele and banjo. He had toured almost one third of the world. Despite the views held by many collectors, Adeler confirms that his band had so far not made any gramophone records. Edgar Adeler and his band went by train to Surabaya in Java but this is how he recalls the story from when they arrived there:

> 'When we reached Surabaya we booked in at the Club where we were engaged to play, and then proceeded down town to enjoy ourselves. There in a first class café accommodating hundreds of guests was a fabulous ten-piece Philippino Jazz Band and who do you think was the featured vocalist? Right first time, Al Bowlly. The lads in the band appealed to me to forgive and forget, but I was adamant. But we did become reconciled before I left Surabaya and were once more on speaking terms and I wished him every good luck for the future.'

CHAPTER FOUR

Blue Skies
1925–27

In Surabaya, Al found himself in the limelight as a singer and banjoist in the café where he continued to earn a good wage. He had found this job by meeting with drummer Dan Hopkins, who not only found him this job, but also fixed him up with somewhere to stay.

Al Bowlly and the band had become so well known that he received an offer from a man called Schwartz, a business man in the entertainment industry who asked him to leave his outfit and come with him to Calcutta's famous Firpo's restaurant where he offered Al a top line job. Al set sail for Calcutta where he signed for one year with Firpo's at an extremely good salary, but within a short space of time, he was to lose all this security.

Al was an inveterate gambler and he could never resist trying to make easy money. Apparently he had got into some heavy gambling sessions whilst in Calcutta and his knuckle-duster had prevented him from being cut down to size. He later told Edgar Adeler that on one occasion he got into a fight with the heavyweight champion boxer of India. The brawl started at the top of a staircase at Al's place of work and by the time they had reached the bottom Al had broken the boxer's jaw. He also admitted that he had got into other fights and had broken another man's jaw at the Calcutta Palais de Dance.

Al Bowlly was emotional, could quickly get involved in scuffles and this time it had cost him his job. And he was penniless. However, being interested in sports, he was able to get work exercising racehorses, pretending in later years he had been a jockey and even claimed to have ridden in the Calcutta races of 1925. To quote from a South African correspondent's letter, when Al's brother Mish eventually heard that he had said this in a press interview he almost fell off his piano stool in fits of laughter! No one then really believed Al was a jockey but in recent years it is just an example of the romance that surrounds the life of Al Bowlly.

He also loved to drive cars although he didn't have one of his own and did not really know how to. A photograph of Al in a car is in the family photo album and on the back is written 'Albert taken in my car. Doesn't he look nice!'

Eventually Al met a Mr S. G. Vickers, then a clerk at the Calcutta branch of Thomas Cook. Vickers introduced him to the French manageress of the Grand Hotel who agreed to let him play in the hotel's café in exchange for room and board.

Not very much time had passed when a large jazz orchestra, led by Jimmy Lequime, a Canadian, opened in the Ballroom of the Grand Hotel, around April 1926. Al walked in and offered his services as vocalist and banjoist, and, after a short audition, got the job as banjoist only, as the band already had a singer.

The Jimmy Lequime Orchestra was a sensation in Calcutta and trumpeter Jimmy became a star. The band did record at the HMV Dum Dum Studios in Calcutta but no recording with an Al Bowlly vocal was made. Meanwhile, the management of the Raffles Hotel in Singapore, hearing of Lequime's success in Calcutta, wrote offering the band a permanent engagement. At the end of 1926 Jimmy Lequime accepted the offer and the band set sail for Singapore.

Jimmy Lequime duly arrived at the Raffles Hotel which, at the time of

Al with the Jimmy Lequime Orchestra, early 1927

Jimmy Lequime and his Orchestra at Calcutta Zoo, 1927

writing remains about the only survivor from those Singapore days of the
1920s music scene. Pianist Monia Liter recalls that the musicians were
treated as guests, having individual suites of rooms, being allowed to eat in
the grill room, etc, etc. Although Lequime originally employed Al as a

banjoist it is now known that as the band's original singer, Pete Harmon, had left, Al had graduated and was a singer at the Raffles Hotel where he used to sing through a megaphone, which Al disliked using. Although the band was successful, it had not been at Raffles very long before it began to break up. Consequently Al left in the spring of 1927 after writing to Edgar Adeler who was now in Europe and renewing their friendship.

Monia Liter urged him to try to get to Europe. Liter was a brilliant pianist with whom Al had become very friendly and who was to play an important part in his life in the 1930s, becoming his personal accompanist. Bowlly wrote a letter to Adeler with which he enclosed a photograph of himself and signed *To Eddie from Al 9.4.1927*, stating that he was humble in his approach, apologising for his foolish misdemeanours that had caused the rift and saying that he was eager to rejoin forces again.

During 1927, Adeler had been playing with the Don Parker band in Oslo and it was around May that he left Oslo and came to Berlin. There he met the German violinist Robert Gaden who had just clinched a three-month contract for a seven-piece band at the select Regina Palast Hotel in Munich. Gaden was in the process of assembling the band; he signed Adeler on piano, Don Barrigo on tenor sax and clarinet, Louis Prager (trumpet); Henri Vandenbosch (trombone); Mario Scanavino (trumpet/violin) and Jeno Obendorfer (drums). Gaden also wanted a vocalist and guitarist for the band and it was thus at a very opportune moment that Bowlly's letter arrived from Singapore. Gaden agreed to sign him on and Adeler cabled Al to leave Singapore at the next opportunity and join them at the Regina Palast, Munich, where the Gaden Band were due to open on 15 May 1927.

Edgar Adeler remembers Al's arrival in Munich:

'I immediately wrote to Al telling him to leave Singapore immediately, advising me full details regarding his departure. He did so, telling me the name of the boat and the Steam Ship Company to which it belonged, viz Messeagies Maritime Marseilles. I then wrote telling him I had posted a letter to Marseilles giving him full instructions and enclosing £10, ample to cover his expenses to Munich. He was to join us there in time to commence the engagement. We duly arrived in Munich, but alas, no Bowlly. We had to start without him, and myself, very upset and embarrassed after my terrific build-up I had given him. But there was nothing to do but carry on. About one week later, I was startled by the sight of a bedraggled Al Bowlly looking like a half starved hobo standing in front of me. He glared at me and for a fleeting moment I stood there immobile, then suddenly with an outburst shouted "What the hell happened to you, Al?" I could see he had gone through hell. He meekly said "I arrived in Marseilles, proceeded to the Messeagies Maritime Office, asked for your letter, and after a diligent search they told me no letter had arrived from you". I cut in and said "That's a bloody disgrace. I checked up so carefully on my letter to you, and it's a scandal that they should have told you that." He was in a flat spin.

Imagine how ghastly, arriving in a foreign country unable to speak the lingo, without a bean to his name, and having to decide what to do. He went to the South African Consul who advanced him his fare to Paris where he told me he had an intro to someone there. But in Paris he struck a dud and then decided to hitch hike to Munich. What an ordeal for anyone to have to undergo. I embraced him, hugged him and told him how my heart bled for him. There MUST be repercussions as I had not failed him and would act drastically against the shipping firm. We fitted him out with some clobber and he started right away. The same old Al Bowlly and an immediate knockout. He had improved beyond measure and my prognostications were fulfilled to the brim.'

Al Bowlly's father died on 24 June 1927, aged 60, after an illness lasting four months. Saxist Don Barrigo recalls that 'there was no laughing or fun on the stand that night. We all felt for Al who was sentimental to a degree.'

The Robert Gaden band with Edgar Adeler and Al Bowlly spent the summer in Munich and it was around the middle of August 1927 that their contract ended and the group disbanded. Al and Don Barrigo who had shared rooms in the Pension Max near the Regina Palast had become firm friends and decided to go to Berlin with Adeler.

One day Edgar Adeler received a re-addressed letter from Marseilles. It was the letter he wrote addressed to Al that was never received. Adeler says that he deliberately opened the letter in the presence of Al and the letter contained the £10 note and full instructions as to the journey to Munich. Adeler was now satisfied in proving to Al that he was not to blame for the non-receipt of the letter, which was found to be properly addressed.

It was not long before Edgar Adeler formed Edgar Adeler and his Hawaiian Quartett (sic) with Bowlly on Hawaiian Guitar. They played all sorts of gigs but were on the look out for more regular work. Adeler became very friendly with Felix 'Tutti' Lehmann, better known as Fred Bird, recording manager for Homocord Records. Bird opened the Homocord doors to Adeler and Bowlly, which started Al off on his recording career.

A recording session was arranged for 18 August 1927 where two numbers were recorded – *Blue Skies* and *Say Mister, Have You met Rosie's Sister?* and issued as a vocal solo by Bowlly with his own ukelele and piano accompaniment by Edgar Adeler. This was Al's first known record. Issued in his own name it was the first in a line of over 600 hundred discs to feature his voice. It has been confirmed that even in 1927, Al Bowlly was displaying the artistry and originality for which he was noted in later years. Both sides of the record prove that he was a competent ukelele player, in particular supplying a hot accompaniment in *Say Mister.*

Adeler recalls at this stage that he wrote a letter to London's Ciro's Club, telling them that he had what he felt was a first class band which had never appeared in England and that he thought would prove a success. In the letter Edgar says that although he had world-beater musicians, the man that he glorified was Al and predicting that he would be a sensation in London. He was very annoyed never to receive a reply or an acknowledgement from Ciro's.

Al stepped into the recording studio for his next session on 12 September 1927 and recorded two vocal choruses with Fred Bird's studio musicians, The Salon Symphonic Jazz Band and this record became Al's first *band* recording as opposed to a solo. Having already recorded one old favourite, *Blue Skies*, he now recorded two more – the ever-popular *Ain't She Sweet* and *In a Little Spanish Town*. More solo records followed during the next few weeks, one of which helped to put Al on the road to success in England and entitled *Muddy Water*. During this time Al recorded both up-tempo numbers such as *Dear Little Gad About* plus slow ballads like *Because I Love You*, illustrating that even in these formative years he was a versatile performer. He was very well received in Berlin and soon managed to build up a reputation. In all he recorded 14 songs in his own right during the Autumn of 1927. Homocord issued publicity material for Al's solo records which contained a sparkling photograph of the new 'singing discovery'. Al also recorded one title vocalising with George Carhart's New Yorkers Jazz Orchestra.

During this time, Bowlly also recorded with Arthur Briggs's Savoy Syncopaters Orchestra on the Deutsche Grammophon label which was the German equivalent to HMV, the label featuring the famous dog and horn gramophone. Briggs's orchestra was considered to be one of the spectacular events in Berlin during 1927 and for many years were erroneously credited as being 'the band who first put the voice of Al Bowlly on record'.

Meanwhile Edgar Adeler received an offer of a one year contract for a seven-piece band at Firpo's Restaurant back in Calcutta. Adeler accepted the offer and cabled back to India that proudly he would be bringing Al Bowlly with him. Firpo's reply was somewhat less encouraging simply saying, DON'T BRING BOWLLY, apparently reflecting Al's reputation in Calcutta the last time he was there.

However, Adeler could not refuse the offer and, in the knowledge that Al was becoming firmly established in Berlin, he left for Calcutta in December 1927.

Al remained in Berlin continuing to record with Fred Bird and Arthur Briggs. In mid-January 1928, he also stepped into the recording studios on three occasions to vocalise with John Abriani and his orchestra. Al Bowlly had become something of a jazz celebrity in Berlin recording both on his own and with the top bands.

Soon, the Fred Rich Band had arrived from London for a three months' engagement at the Wintergarten, Berlin, opening on 6 February 1928. During this engagement, it is now thought that Al Bowlly joined the band as

A portrait of Al taken in Singapore, 1927

vocalist but in mid-April, and prior to the end of the contract, Fred Rich secretly returned to the USA leaving his orchestra stranded in Berlin.

In the meantime a saxophonist from Britain named Billy Bartholomew was forming a small group of his own to play at the Eden Hotel in Berlin. The group The Eden Five played there from 1 October 1927 to 30 April of the following year. After this contract had ended, Bartholomew enlarged his group to full orchestra size by integrating a number of musicians from the former Fred Rich Band, including Al Bowlly as singer.

The enlarged band was assembled for an engagement at the newly-opened Delphi Palast, Berlin, from 1 May to mid-June 1928 and was christened Billy Bartholomew's Delphians Jazz Band.

During this period the Delphians made a number of recordings, the majority of which have still not been traced. However, from the catalogues issued at the time it appears that Al sung on round about a dozen of these. One that has been traced and contains a good vocal refrain by Al is entitled *Changes* and it has already found its way onto a vintage jazz LP issued in Germany.

During this period Bowlly received a communication from Len Fillis who had made a name for himself in England. He was then guitarist with Fred Elizalde's band at the Savoy Hotel in London and he informed Al that there was a vacancy in the band for a singer. If Al could land this job singing to the patrons at the Savoy, all his ambitions would be fulfilled! As an audition he sent over the record he had made of *Muddy Water* and back came the reply from the Spanish band leader Elizalde – an offer of a job with the band at a wage of £14 a week. This was less than he had been earning on the continent. So Al gambled and wrote to Fred Elizalde demanding more money. Fortunately for Al, despite the fact that he was virtually unknown in England, Elizalde agreed, even sending him an advance of £20 to pay his fare from Germany to England.

We have already seen that Al was a sportsman and liked to gamble. Money did not mean very much to him; he was not a business man and all through his career he never really had a good manager. This all meant that money slipped through his hands like water. He would spend it on cigarettes (at times he smoked very heavily), gifts and loans to friends which were often not paid back. Al rarely saved any money, his philosophy being to 'live for today'. The only form of investment that he currently embarked upon was gambling and often he would gamble away his last few shillings in a desperate hope to make money. This is what he did, in effect, when Fred Elizalde offered him a job and Al wrote back asking for more money since not being known in England could have lost him the job. This time, however, the gamble paid off. But when Elizalde sent him the £20 advance of salary Al himself tells us (and this could well be another fable which Bowlly himself initiated) that he spent £5 of this on entertaining friends and put the rest on a horse – and lost his money.

Al Bowlly was generous to a fault; he would give the shirt off his back if he thought it was a deserving case, although frequently his generosity was not returned to him. Fortunately, just when he needed it the most, his generosity was returned, for on this occasion a friend offered to lend him the money for first class travel from Germany to London and enough to pay his hotel bills at either end of the journey. This offer saved the day as far as Al was concerned, and after arriving in London he scrimped and saved, living in inferior accommodation in order to pay back the loan.

CHAPTER FIVE

Time on my Hands
1928–29

After Al's arrival in London in July 1928, Fred Elizalde became the first bandleader in England to employ Al Bowlly and he did so both as vocalist and guitarist. Al's first record in England was *Just Imagine* coupled with a hot number *Wherever you are* billed on the label simply as Fred Elizalde and his Music, with vocal refrain.

Among those in the Elizalde band were Harry Hayes, Rex Owen, Adrian Rollini and Len Fillis.

Fred Elizalde was a genius and he brought a wealth of experience from the field of classical music into the dance and jazz scene of the 1920s. This was invaluable to dance music which was in the stages of evolving from Dixieland Jazz and Elizalde's band was the most advanced group playing in Britain at the time.

As July 1928 drew to a close, Al Bowlly returned to the continent again for three months with Elizalde. Their first engagement was Paris where they opened at Les Ambassadeurs Restaurant in the Champs-Elysées with a 19-piece band.

The other band playing at the restaurant was the Noble Sissle Orchestra. Al got on famously with the French musicians and even sang a few numbers with Noble Sissle who liked his style. Then the Elizalde band moved on to the Casino, Ostend, but the band were not allowed to gamble there – much to Al's dismay! However, he soon found his way to the sea front each day where he passed his time away on the beach. Incidentally, the band did find somewhere to gamble! The stay in Ostend lasted six weeks and in October 1928 the Fred Elizalde band crossed the Channel and returned to the Savoy Hotel where they stayed for a further eight months.

During their stay at the Savoy, the band made frequent broadcasts over the BBC, but the sound quality of these were very poor and it was not until January 1929 that, after many complaints, a second microphone was installed to improve the sound balance. Unfortunately Al Bowlly came over badly in the broadcasts; his high notes appeared to waver and he could do himself no justice at all. Late in April 1929, the band had a three week engagement at the London Palladium in which Al was the featured vocalist. But once again, he could not do himself justice with this orchestra.

Fred Elizalde and his Music, 1928

On 23 June, the Fred Elizalde band took part in a concert organised by the *Melody Maker* at the Shepherd's Bush Pavilion, where again Bowlly provided many vocals. Apart from the record already mentioned, Al made a further five titles with the Elizalde band. In the main these records did not really suit Al's voice either and additionally were poor recordings as the company for which most of them were made, Brunswick, did not have its own, or indeed any permanent recording studio at that time.

Fred Elizalde was a hot-tempered person and he had recurring rows with the management of the Savoy Hotel. These were over the kind of music that

should be played – Elizalde wanting predominantly *hot* music whilst the Savoy wanted the emphasis on *sweet* music. Consequently Elizalde's contract, which expired on 31 July 1929, was not renewed. He did not form another band in this country and shortly afterwards went abroad.

During his stay at the Savoy Hotel, Bowlly did a little freelancing in the recording studios. On 6 November 1928 he was paid two guineas for supplying ukelele accompaniment to the Trix Sisters.

Apart from this and making a few records with 'Fred Elizalde and his Music', Al had also made one with Van Phillips, two with Percival Mackey

37

and one with Len Fillis under his pseudonym 'Linn Milford'. Nevertheless, these jobs did not pay very well and despite his regular salary from Elizalde, he now had very little money and was redundant.

The remainder of the summer was a very lean time for Al and in this period he is reputed to have actually busked in the streets of London in order to make ends meet. In a 1938 press interview Al recalled, 'For several mornings I stood at the corner and sang softly to the passing crowds. Sometimes a word of sympathy was given with an odd copper or two. But nobody knew me. I pulled my coat collar up round my ears in case I should be recognised.' This occurred in Piccadilly near an underground station and he apparently earned £2.17s in this undignified pursuit. Although Al has a reputation for story telling in press interviews, most researchers believe the busking episode actually took place.

Al's next musical engagement occurred in the autumn of 1929 when he became a part time member of a local London band led by Ernie Rutterford. Ernie Rutterford and his band were doing one night stands at Masonic Ladies nights and similar functions at such places as the Connaught Room, Holborn Restaurant, Dorchester, Savoy, Park Lane and other hotels. The band was also engaged by the *Sunday League* for stage shows at theatres on their circuit which included the Palladium, Finsbury Park Empire and Hackney Empire.

Rutterford's trumpeter, Bill Outlaw, who now lives in retirement in Essex recalls how Al got the job in the band:

> 'We were playing at a dinner in the West End where members of the profession – including Al – were present, when one, I think an agent, asked Ernie to let Al sing a number with the band. This was his introduction to us and Ernie booked him for our Sunday League Concerts and some Masonics etc.'

At this time the microphone and amplification was not available to assist Al's vocals with Ernie Rutterford. The band's drummer, Bert Davenport, now recalls the following incident:

> 'I remember distinctly that during a rehearsal Al asked my wife to go the rear of the theatre to hear whether his voice came over – and she had to say that she could not hear him very well. She suggested that he might try a megaphone. This he did and it was found to be fairly successful. In fact he used a megaphone for most of the shows afterwards. How different from the amplification used today by bands and groups!'

Davenport remembers how Al used to squeeze into his old Austin car together with the drum kit and that was the way they travelled from show to show. 'He was a great guy,' recalls Bert, 'very carefree and nothing seemed to disturb him.' The fact that Al was a carefree and happy-go-lucky person is reiterated by Bill Outlaw who recollects a couple of incidents illustrating the point:

'I remember being in the band's dressing room at a Sunday League Concert near the time to go on. Al came rushing in, "Sorry Ernie, I cannot stay – I have a most pressing engagement with Len Fillis." You can imagine this caused panic stations momentarily but these were soon dispelled when he grinned, took off his coat, enjoying the leg pull and proceeded to give an excellent performance with us on stage. At the conclusion of another Sunday League Concert, we took our customary "curtains" then Ernie took his personal one in front of the curtain. Al was fooling around behind the curtain, posing as a ballet dancer when the curtain suddenly went up much to the amusement of the audience.'

In one Sunday League Concert, at the Kingston Empire, The Ernie Rutterford Band were playing *I'm happy when I'm hiking.* In order to inject some comedy into the corn, Al appeared with his hair parted in the middle and pulled down over his ears. His trousers were rolled up to reveal a pair of 'jazzy' socks and suspenders!

During this period he also did freelance recording work, especially during 1930. But in 1929, even this work had been scarce with nothing since the spring of that year until November when he stepped into the Regal studios for another 'Linn Milford' session. One of the numbers recorded at this session was *Lay My Head beneath a Rose* which despite its morbid sentiment is really beautifully sung and the disc presents his voice to an advantage not previously captured on record. Curiously enough, this record had a 'barber-shop quartet' sound about it!

Meanwhile, Len Fillis had been appearing in a dance orchestra in the Piccadilly Hotel. He had previously done much stage work and the lure of the footlights drew him again when he left the Piccadilly Hotel with plans to form a trio soon to be known as the Blue Boys. Len invited Edgar Adeler, who had recently arrived in England, and Al Bowlly to join him in this venture. At the last minute Al Starita, a well-known London dance band musician, came on the scene and the trio became a quartet.

When the story of the formation of the Blue Boys was reported in the *Melody Maker*, the reporter stated 'Al CAN sing, given a fair opportunity.' This serves to emphasize the fact he had made little impact with Elizalde and that he was virtually unknown in England still despite having sung at the Savoy Hotel.

In the above-mentioned article it is reported that in the Blue Boys, Al Bowlly and Edgar Adeler were to play two pianos. Bowlly was also going to dance and play guitar, and all four were to sing.

CHAPTER SIX

Something to Sing About
1929–30

Having formed the Blue Boys it was decided to concentrate on the provinces until the act became polished. Al Starita and Len Fillis were already known in the West End dance music world whilst Edgar Adeler and Al Bowlly were practically unknown. Edgar wrote to D. J. Clarke, a friend of his father's, who was proprietor of two theatres, and on the strength of this, the quartet got their first week's booking at the Argyle Theatre at Birkenhead starting 20 January 1930, followed by a week in Northern Ireland.

The Blue Boys' offerings were well received in Birkenhead but not a howling success, probably due to the fact that the act was still raw. However, they were much better received in Belfast by the local dance band fans. The group had an official welcoming at one of the leading restaurants and soon the jazz fans revered the names of Starita and Fillis.

This engagement was followed up with an engagement in Keighley, where the Boys flopped as the previous week's top of the bill was an accordion band which had brought the house down and obviously this was the type of act that appealed to the audience there.

Nevertheless, they continued working, appearing at various venues including such places as the Pleasure Gardens, Folkestone, and featuring such hits of the day as *Tip-toe through the Tulips* and *Am I Blue?* And what is almost forgotten is that the three of the Blue Boys who were known in South Africa (Bowlly, Fillis and Adeler) took time off to make a short film of their act for showing in South Africa. This was almost certainly the first cinema film in which Al Bowlly appeared. Although no copy has been traced to confirm whether or not Al sings in it, it seems highly likely that he did.

The life of the Blue Boys was, unfortunately, a short one, lasting only a month or so. Edgar Adeler tells the remaining story of the quartet:

> 'As far as stage presentation was concerned Starita and Fillis were non-starters. It was the unknown Al Bowlly and Edgar Adeler who got all the limelight. The two of us were showmen whereas Len and Starita lacked that touch of stagecraft which we two outsiders obviously enjoyed. But combined with their West End glamour we just couldn't fail. However, there was one snag. Al Starita was an American of Italian stock; Al Bowlly was a South African of Lebanese stock. Both with a

touch of continental flare-up temperaments. To avoid any possibility of a clash between the two opposites we always had two dressing rooms, one for Bowlly and myself, and t'other for Starita and Len. This worked like magic but was too good to last. The day came when we realised our ambition. We signed a contract with the famous Scots comedian Harry Gordon for a summer season at his Aberdeen venue at £120 a week. Then came the deathblow. At a one-night stand in Aldershot with the Rupert Ingelese Roadshow, Len Fillis rushed into our dressing room and said "Come on Edgar hurry up. There's trouble between the two Als." And there we discovered Al Starita towering over Al Bowlly with a soda water bottle raised to his head and Al Bowlly with a knife to his adversary's throat. We managed to separate them but that was the end of the Blue Boys. We cancelled our contract with Harry Gordon, who was the perfect gentleman, and realised how futile it was for us to carry on.'

Also during this Blue Boys period, Adeler recalls that Len Fillis had a recording session booked with the Regal Company and invited Adeler, Bowlly and Al Starita to form a group for this session to be known as The Regal Quartet. The recording manager wanted a record with an Afrikaans vocal to be the first in a series to be sent over to South Africa. He knew that Al Bowlly could sing in this language. The record was duly cut and sent to South Africa but was rejected as Al's Afrikaans had too much of a Lebanese accent!

Unless a copy of this rejected record remains in archives somewhere or a copy of the Blue Boys film can be traced, there will be no sound evidence of the Blue Boys as they did not make any commercial records as such.

Al had achieved some success with Elizalde and the Blue Boys but he was still definitely not established in England. Len Fillis had coached him further in guitar playing and by now he had become a competent rhythm guitarist, pianist and banjo player. On one occasion during rehearsals for a provincial appearance Al took the pianist's seat and demonstrated the kind of accompaniment he required, which was flowery runs. In fact, Al was as good a guitarist and pianist as he needed to be but not, of course, in the same class as Len Fillis or Monia Liter.

From the break up of the Blue Boys around the end of February 1930, Al drifted somewhat into obscurity. Although he had no regular work, he did a lot of freelance work in the recording studio, recording almost 100 titles in this way. In particular he recorded with such leaders as Jay Wilbur, Alfredo, Marius B. Winter and Harry Hudson, also continuing to freelance in the studio with Len Fillis throughout 1930 and into 1931.

During the late 1920s and early 1930s, Len Fillis made numerous records on various labels under his own name and names such as 'Honolulu Serenaders', 'Brooklyn Broadcasters', 'Linn Milford and his Hawaiians', 'Al Vocale', 'Ferrachini' and several others. On many of these Fillis used a vocal

Len Fillis, who knew Al from his South Africa days now provided Al with much freelance recording work

duet and often this was between Les Allen and Al Bowlly, occasionally both were allowed a solo spot. Sometimes, however, Al would just play guitar. Les Allen, being asked in the 1970s if he remembers recording with Al, said that he did, but knew nothing of Al's private life. On leaving the recording studio, they would both go their separate ways.

Back to 1930; Al did not earn very much from the freelancing. Indeed, in August of that year he was a guest at a friend's wedding at the Bloomsbury Palace Hotel in London's Russell Square, but Al, unfortunately, could not afford a present. Instead he offered the one thing he was most able to offer – his voice – and got onto the bandstand to sing a couple of numbers at the reception.

It is also interesting to note that in June 1930, Al stepped into the studio for the first time in England as a soloist and recorded a couple of titles for HMV. These were, however, for the South African market and sung in Afrikaans! He went on to record some more Afrikaan titles on the Decca label.

The very next month, Bowlly arrived at the recording studio once again to provide the vocals on three numbers by the Night Club Kings who were directed by Ray Noble. Unfortunately, HMV rejected all these recordings, although later in the year the group recorded two of them again – but with a

Les Allen, who frequently duetted with Al on the recording sessions arranged by Len Fillis in the early 1930s

different singer! Ray Noble was director of the HMV house band and was destined to play a very important part in the up and coming career of Al Bowlly.

Noble was a talented young pianist/arranger/composer who had won a *Melody Maker* dance band arranging competition and afterwards found himself staff arranger for Jack Payne's BBC Dance Orchestra and had taken over direction of the HMV house band in 1929 from Carroll Gibbons. This house band was known as the New Mayfair Dance Orchestra and its musicians were drawn from top London dance bands, the function of which was to accompany HMV artistes and also to make records in their own right.

Some four months after Al had made the rejected Night Club Kings recordings, Ray Noble invited him to sing some numbers with his full dance orchestra. It was in November of 1930 that Al Bowlly first became Noble's band·singer with the New Mayfair Dance Orchestra. The titles recorded were *I'm telling the World She's Mine* and *How could I be Lonely?* and they

Ray Noble, leader of the houseband at HMV for whom Al provided most of the vocal refrains from November 1930 to August 1934

are excellent examples of Al's singing and both Ray Noble and HMV were suitably impressed.

Before Al sung with Noble's band, Ray asked him if he sang in the printed key. Being anxious to record with Noble, Al said 'yes' immediately and it was not until some months later that Noble realised Al's true range was about one third lower.

At first Al shared the vocal work in the Noble band with Jack Plant, a popular band singer of the era, but it wasn't long before Al Bowlly became the regular vocalist for the house band at HMV.

This was then the start of what was probably the greatest combination in British dance music history. Noble and Bowlly went on to make well over 200 recordings using this orchestra that was, except for rare occasions, purely a recording band that never existed outside the HMV studios.

However, Ray Noble had a terrific influence at HMV. Whoever he wanted in his band, he was able to engage over whoever else may have wanted the particular musician. Among the musicians who played in the Noble band over the years were such leading men as: Max Goldberg, Jack Jackson and Nat Gonella (trumpets); Bert Thomas (guitar); Spike Hughes and Tiny Winters (string bass); Billy Reid (piano accordion); Bill Harty (drums); Monia Liter (piano) and Freddy Gardner (clarinet).

During 1930, Al became quite well-known in the recording studios, sufficiently so for Decca to invite him to record three solo titles (one being the famous blues *Frankie and Johnny*) in November of that year, assisted by popular female vocalist Ella Logan. It would be the next two years which were to be the most prolific for Al Bowlly on records, for he would not only have a regular job with a recording band, but would freelance as well.

Although Al appeared in the recording studios with Ray Noble, Len Fillis, Harry Hudson and a few other bandleaders, these were only freelance jobs. However, towards the end of 1930, Noble's drummer Bill Harty had some news that raised Al's hopes of getting a regular job.

Harty was then working with American bandleader Roy Fox who had been brought over to play at the Café de Paris. Although Roy's engagement there had ended, he had been awarded the contract to lead a recording band for Decca and was looking for a new vocalist. But, unlike Noble, Fox had plans for his band to work regularly both in and out of the recording studio. Bill Harty arranged for Al to meet Roy Fox at the Coventry Street offices of Ralph Dean. Al Bowlly asked Roy Fox to listen to the record he had brought with him which was the first one he had made with Ray Noble, recorded a few weeks earlier. After hearing both sides of the record, Roy told Al that he would be hearing from him. Al was still desperately trying to impress the American bandleader, and with less than £3 in his pocket he invited Mr and Mrs Fox for lunch at a nearby restaurant.

After lunch, Al went across to the bandleader playing to the patrons and following a hurried conversation, got up with the band and sang *I Love the Moon* plus a couple of jazzy numbers. When Al returned to his table Roy Fox said simply 'OK you get the job!' Al pressed Roy into giving him written confirmation of the engagement, which he did, and to Al's delight the salary placed him among London's highest paid dance band vocalists.

The above description, at least, is what Al told of his audition afterwards in the article entitled 'My Life of Song' for the magazine *Radio Pictorial* in 1938. However, another version is told in Roy Fox's autobiography *Hollywood, Mayfair and all that Jazz*. Here, it simply says that Al was introduced to Roy Fox and pianist Lew Stone accompanied Al at the audition. No mention of gramophone records or lunch at a restaurant thus illustrating another myth surrounding the life of Al Bowlly.

Roy Fox had played with and had led bands in California, Miami and New York. He became musical director for the Fox Film Studios (no relation) and while in this capacity, he received the invitation to come to London. The band for which he recruited Al Bowlly was one of stars and Roy was destined to become one of Britain's top-notch band leaders.

CHAPTER SEVEN

You're Lucky to Me
1931–32

The Roy Fox Band commenced recording in January 1931 but since it was still only a recording band, Al still had no regular daily engagement. Al's first record with Fox was made on 5 January 1931, the titles being *You're Lucky to Me* and *Thank Your Father*, the vocalist on the label being mistakenly credited as Kenneth Allen, Fox's ex-singer from the Café de Paris. During Al's time with Roy Fox, which lasted over the next 20 months, over 150 titles were recorded on the Decca label and all but a handful featured the voice of Al Bowlly. Many of these were marred by poor quality of sound with noisy surfaces and muffled vocals. The balance was often faulty and the top frequencies (i.e. *s* sounds) were missing. In fact, those who heard the band in the flesh generally say the records were a poor representation.

This is how Roy Fox remembered Al in a post-war interview:

'Al and I became close friends. He was charming and a very happy man. He was a very fine vocalist and had a feeling for a song. Above all, he had a terrific personality – so likeable. Really could put a song over. Nice smart appearance, handsome. I was lucky to have him in the band.'

Roy Fox continued to make records for Decca but he did not get his first big break until the spring of 1931. Jack Upson, who was managing director of the Dolcis Shoe Company was branching out by opening a smart restaurant in Piccadilly which he called The Monseigneur and, having heard many of the West End bands, he decided to offer Roy Fox the contract to be the restaurant's regular bandleader. There was no audition despite the popular belief that there was one at which Al sung, among other things, *Goodnight Sweetheart*. This story eminated, as many have done, from what Al told the press during the 1930s.

The Roy Fox Band opened at the Monseigneur Restaurant on 27 May 1931. Al Bowlly was so grateful for his pay after his first week's work that he took Roy and Dorothea Fox for a meal in a little Italian restaurant in Soho. Roy Fox recalls an anecdote which occurred during this meal:

'During the course of the delicious chicken entree I thought I heard a most peculiar kind of sound. After much detective work, I discovered Al was chewing on a chicken bone. I queried this and he said, "Boss (he always called me Boss), haven't you tried chewing chicken bones? They're the best part and very good for the teeth." Well, I knew Al had beautiful white teeth, but I never realised how he kept them looking that way.'

The Monseigneur Restaurant itself became something of a legend and was opened not so much on a profit motive but as a means by which the owner could entertain his friends. The decor was unusually beautiful and as money was of little concern, Upson employed the best artists and musicians he could get and the hospitality was lavish.

Once settled at the Monseigneur Restaurant, the Roy Fox Band became one of the highlights of London's night life. Playing in the band were several musicians that were later to achieve success in their own right, in particular Lew Stone, Spike Hughes and Nat Gonella. The quality of the music and especially the presence of Bowlly attracted many of the West End Society people to come and listen and dance to the music. Arrangements were soon made for them to broadcast weekly from 10.30pm to midnight every Tuesday on the late night dance music programmes put out by the BBC. Thus the fame of both the band and Bowlly spread. Al Bowlly soon became a well-known name among those in the entertainment world and members of the public who took an interest in popular music.

The band would also do 'Ciné-Variety' which was stage appearances between films at cinemas. They opened in 'Ciné-Variety' at the Paramount Cinema in Regent Street.

Al was now really in his element; he had a regular job in a band that was one of the West End's main attractions. And when he was not singing with Roy Fox each night at the Monseigneur, he would be due at the recording studios to record either with Fox, Ray Noble or a host of other bands who required his services on a freelance basis.

Up until then, Al had no full-time engagements, only recording work. 1931 was to be Al's busiest year in the recording studios, singing the vocal refrains of well over 200 titles. Needless to say, he had to have a good memory for the lyrics, and on occasions was spotted at the Monseigneur Restaurant holding a piece of paper in the palm of his hand whilst singing, on which were written, in tiny writing, the words of a new song!

Among the notables Al recorded with during his Roy Fox period were Elsie Carlisle and Billy Cotton, whose band played good jazz before his *Wakey-Wakey* image. Others included top clarinettist Sid Phillips, and the beloved Carroll Gibbons, so fondly remembered for his long association with the Savoy Hotel. Al can be heard on many of the Savoy Hotel Orpheans' records from the 1931–2 period including many issued under the name The Masqueraders.

Above:
Al, sporting a moustache,
with Roy Fox and his
Band at the Monseigneur
Restaurant in 1931

Left:
Roy Fox, who gave Al his
first really big break in
England in January 1931

Billy Cotton, with whom Al made just the one record, in 1931

Carroll Gibbons, beloved leader of the Savoy Hotel Orpheans with whom Al sung, mainly during 1932

By this time, Al had moved into a flat in Cranbourne Mansions, Charing Cross Road. It was a small flat and as Al travelled light and had few personal possessions, those who visited recall that it never looked 'lived-in'. However, with all the work he was now getting he was able to move into better accommodation at No 17 Orange Street, Piccadilly. He even opened an account at the Leicester Square branch of the National Provincial Bank. A subsequent internal bank memo reads '. . . client . . . being described as a musician (Roy Fox's Band). He was actually a "crooner" and was fairly well known.'

Life was now one big round of hard work, with rehearsals and recording during the day, plus a night's work at the Monseigneur. But Al was strong – he could take it, and because he never tired of singing he loved his work. His voice was his main interest in life, and with physical culture his second passion, he was well qualified for the hectic life he was now living.

During this period in the history of popular music, many people held the view that singers, or 'crooners' as they were then known, like Al Bowlly, were representative of the 'soft and decadent youth'. One anecdote that Al later recalled was that he once heard someone making offensive remarks about crooning while Al was singing. At the end of his vocal he went over to this person and felled him with one blow. Obviously this particular individual realised to his cost that Al Bowlly was not a representative of the soft and decadent youth! But another Bowlly myth, almost certainly!

50

As the popularity of the Roy Fox Band grew, so did the popularity of Al Bowlly, as he was now recognised as one of Britain's top band singers. This was acknowledged by Decca. Up to then, Al's name had not appeared on the label of any of the records he had made with Roy Fox. However, in June 1931 an internal Decca memorandum concerning a recording session by Roy Fox reads 'Vocal refrain by Al Bowlly – type to be as large as possible'. But by September, the legendary 'with vocal refrain' is all that appeared once again on the Fox/Bowlly records. This coincided with Al being asked by Decca again to make some records as a soloist – so there may be some connection there.

Apart from the Afrikaans recordings already mentioned, and three titles recorded for Decca in November 1930 and issued sometime later, Al's first regular solo recording work began in September 1931 when he recorded *Were You Sincere* and *I'd Rather Be a Beggar with You*. Al went on to make many solo records during his career, firstly on Decca and later on HMV.

During 1931, Roy Fox went sick and his illness took him away from the

Elsie Carlisle with whom Al duetted in *Songs from the Shows*

51

Al and Freda Bowlly on their wedding day, 18th December 1931

West End music scene. His doctor ordered a complete rest-cure in Switzerland where he went in October 1931 and remained until the following spring. Fox asked the band's pianist, Lew Stone, to take over direction and leadership while he was away in Switzerland and the musical press at the time gave Lew full credit for improving and popularising the band.

It was in December 1931 in the nearby Lyons Corner House that trumpeter Nat Gonella introduced Al to a well-known 18-year-old local girl, Freda Roberts, the daughter of a merchant seaman. She was born in Yorkshire and according to Gonella she 'had a reputation'. Al, not knowing her and having very little guile, fell for her and on 18 December 1931 married her in the St Martin Register Office, London. None of the boys in the band expected him to be serious about her, let alone marry her, for he was so popular in the West End that he could have virtually had the pick of any woman. But he calmly announced to the band shortly after the event, 'I got married today' – the bandsmen were stunned and were not really surprised when they learned a few weeks later that the marriage had broken up. The story goes that Al returned to his flat after work one evening to discover his pretty young wife with another man. This was a terrible blow for Al and the whole band felt bad about it, for although professional musicians were often noted for their earthy way of living, Al was really the exception. Although the marriage broke up in January 1932, it was not until January 1934 that his divorce was finalised after Freda had sued Al for adultery. For a few years after they parted, Freda was seen around the clubs and restaurants in the West End of London with various escorts, later turning to drugs and drink and, like so many others who came to the attention of the public in the 1930s, eventually drifting into obscurity.

During 1931, Lew Stone, the pianist/arranger with the Roy Fox Band, became musical director for the British and Dominion Picture Company. One of the earliest films for which Lew did the music arranging was *A Night Like This* starring Ralph Lynn, Tom Walls and Robertson Hare, released in 1932. In this film Lew Stone can be seen in several sequences conducting a band consisting of Roy Fox's men in which Al sang one or two numbers including *In London on a Night Like This* which he sang through a megaphone. Recordings were made at the time by Al with Fox's men under the pseudonym of The Rhythm Maniacs. Two other numbers from this film were *Considering* and *Hello Mike* which Al recorded with Arthur Lally and his orchestra.

In March 1932 Al, having dual nationality, was issued with a British passport. However, typical of Al, he lost it the very next year.

Roy Fox came back to the Monseigneur in April 1932 to find his band 'second to none in London' to quote from the magazine *The Gramophone*. Although he was under doctor's advice to take things easy, Roy became very busy and one of the first jobs he accepted was an offer to appear with the band at the London Palladium. This show was given good reviews by the musical press.

Also in 1932, the Roy Fox Band could be seen on the silver screen, this time in its own right with Fox conducting in a Pathé short in which the band played a comedy song of the day entitled *It Ain't No Fault of Mine*. Nat Gonella was featured vocalist on this, although Al can quite clearly be seen playing rhythm guitar. The Fox band with Al appeared in another Pathé clip in which they accompany cabaret artiste Douglas Byng. Again, Al is only seen, not heard.

Roy Fox's contract with the Monseigneur was shortly due to end and it was decided by mutual agreement that it should not be renewed. The management of the restaurant then looked around the West End to find a replacement, and eventually asked Lew Stone to form a band. After a little hesitation he accepted the offer.

The members of the Roy Fox band, with the exception of Al Bowlly were under contract to the Monseigneur, and apart from trumpeter Sid Buckman they all elected to remain at the Monseigneur under the baton of Lew Stone. This included Al Bowlly who was actually under contract to Roy Fox. Legal proceedings were instituted between Fox and Bowlly with Roy obtaining a temporary injunction on 22 October restraining Al from breaking his contract. However, on 25 October at a hearing in chambers the judge denied Fox's application for the injunction to be made permanent on the grounds that the contract was not sufficiently explicit. The matter was resolved out of court and Lew Stone with Al Bowlly as vocalist opened at the Monseigneur on 24 October 1932.

Left:
John Watt, famed for his *Songs from the Shows* series in the 1930s. Al sung just two titles with John

Right:
Nat Gonella who worked alongside Al in the bands led by Roy Fox and Lew Stone

"Tiny" Winters.

Left:
Tiny Winters, the personality bassist
with Lew Stone's Band

Below:
Al at the microphone with Lew Stone
and his Band

CHAPTER EIGHT

My Hat's on the Side of My Head

1932–34

The new band was billed as 'Lew Stone and the Monseigneur Dance Orchestra'; the music became more sophisticated and the band even more popular than its predecessors. Lew took a very special interest in Al, giving him the direction and encouragement he needed with his arrangements, taking into consideration his vocal range, etc, perhaps more so than any other leader with whom he worked. The Lew Stone band was a compact and friendly unit and all the musicians enjoyed playing in it. Each member was given a nick-name beginning with the name 'Joe' – Al became known as 'Joe Sex'.

'Al was a hard worker and always punctual', recalled Tiny Winters, the band's bass player; however, he was late on one occasion and offered an excuse that no one believed, that he had to mend gaskets on a friend's car on the Great West Road. He could be very boyish at times, according to Tiny who also remembers that Al drank very little – 'He could not take it'.

The first record made by the Lew Stone band with Al Bowlly was *Nightfall* and *Rain, Rain Go Away* recorded in October 1932. This was the first in a long line of well over 100 titles recorded from 1932 to 1938 by Lew with Al Bowlly. And nearly all these were superior to those he had made with previous bandleaders, Fred Elizalde and Roy Fox. To give him a chance to concentrate on his singing as far as the band's recording work was concerned, Al was relieved of his guitar playing duties by various other guitarists, among whom was Bill Herbert, who is best remembered for his long association with the Billy Cotton Band Show on radio and TV.

The Lew Stone band took over the BBC's late night dance music programme from 10.30pm to midnight every Tuesday. Lew Stone was, indeed, a very important person in dance band history in Britain, both historically and musically. He had previously arranged for such bandleaders as Bert Ralton and Ambrose as well as for Roy Fox and his arrangements were considered among the most advanced and inventive of the era. The name 'Al Bowlly' soon became synonymous with the name 'Lew Stone', as Lew always gave Al credit for vocal refrains.

By 1933 Al had reached the peak of his career in England being cited frequently by the popular press as 'Bing Crosby's most dangerous rival'. For example, in the *News Chronicle* of 27 February 1933 he is referred to as the 'supreme crooner in this country'. This reference was in connection with a dance band competition organised by that newspaper which commenced with the issue of one English and one American record. On the English record was featured Jack Hylton on one side and Lew Stone with Al Bowlly on the other, both singer and band having equal billing on the record label. The American record featured Wayne King on one side and Guy Lombardo with Bing Crosby on the other side, again singer and band having equal billing. The competition was for members of the public to guess the sales of each record. The sales in 1933 were certified by a firm of chartered accountants as being nearly 28,000 for the English record and nearly 20,000 for the American one.

Al did not just record and broadcast with Lew Stone. Lew toured the country topping the bill with stage appearances as was becoming fashionable with the dance bands. In fact Al had the honour of singing to royalty with Lew at the London Palladium.

The band's first provincial appearance was in Yorkshire on 13 February 1933 and from then on the band started to be seen by those who had

Lew Stone and his Band

previously only listened to them on the radio or bought the records. The band, and in particular Al, received much praise from the critics. To quote from Stanley Nelson, music critic of *Era*, when the band appeared at the London Palladium in 1933:

> 'The hit of the show was of course Al Bowlly. His rendering of the Jewish number *A letter to my mother* stopped the show. He sung into the microphone and his voice was amplified through the theatre. I have expressed myself on the subject of Al's singing before. He is pre-eminently a microphone singer. There is no denying his personality which he can put over microphonically as well as anyone here, and he has a feeling for rhythm which is second only to Bing Crosby. But right or wrong, I consider Billy Scott-Coomber a better all round vocalist. Yet, and I must be fair, he was the highspot of the Palladium show, a fact to which Lew Stone rather charmingly acquiesced on the stage.'

Of course, the band's stage act had to be made more visual than hitherto. For example, in one number about a rag and bone man, *Junk Man Blues*, Al would come on stage pushing a barrow. Tiny Winters recalls an anecdote in

Al with popular girl singer, Pat Hyde

At the Monseigneur Restaurant with Lew Stone and his Band

which the barrow got jammed in the wings just as Al was about to wheel it out in front of the audience at the Holborn Empire. The band had to vamp for some while until the barrow was freed and Al was able to push it out on to the stage.

The stage appearances did increase the band's popularity. Both Lew and Al got enormous fan mail. Consequently, in April 1933, when the *Melody Maker* published the list of musicians whose photographs were in the most demand, out of the 12 listed, six were members of Lew Stone's band, and top of the list was Al Bowlly.

It is worth mentioning that in this early 1933 Lew Stone period, Boosey and Hawkes produced a lightweight roll-up megaphone for vocalists which the makers claimed was designed by Al Bowlly. The megaphone, incidentally, sold for 14s 3d. This was strange because Al Bowlly disliked using a megaphone saying among other things that they hid the singer's face preventing him from expressing any form of personality.

More films followed to feature the Lew Stone band for the British and Dominion Company, for whom Lew was still musical director. In particular, in 1933 the band appeared in *The Mayor's Nest* starring Sydney Howard and Claude Hulbert. As the credits flashed on the screen the magic words 'Al Bowlly' could be seen.

When he appeared, however, Al was hardly the Monseigneur Bowlly, in

Monia Liter,
Al's brilliant
pianist

fact he depicted 'George', an itinerant musician. Seated with Sydney
Howard on a doorstep, and watching some children enact a mock wedding,
Al sang *Wedding of the Slum Town Babies* in his own individual way. In a
later scene Al was up before the magistrate in a courtroom scene where he
had the entire personnel of the court joining in with a typical cheer-up song
entitled *Say to Yourself, I Will Be Happy*. This is the only feature film in
which Al had an acting part. His appearance lasted no more than about three
minutes in total, including the two above-mentioned songs. The Lew Stone
band continued to appear in other British and Dominion films, but Al did not

have a solo spot in these. He could be heard singing such numbers as *Antoinette* and *What More Can I Ask?* In Noel Coward's *Bitter Sweet*, which starred Anna Neagle, Al can be seen with the band playing guitar for about 12 seconds right at the end of the film.

Al had a cigarette in his mouth for his whole appearance in *Bitter Sweet* highlighting the fact he was quite a heavy smoker. On many occasions when he was photographed he was also smoking, whether at the race track, in a recording studio, in a restaurant or talking to an agent! (On the subject of drinking, both Ray Noble and Tiny Winters remember Al drinking only very moderately.)

Whilst appearing on the stage with Lew Stone, Al had been spotted by impressario Val Parnell of Moss Empires, who believed in Al so much that he decided to give him the chance of appearing on the Halls in his own right as a solo variety artiste. This he did and Al made his debut on 11 September 1933 at the Holborn Empire where he shared top billing with Louis Armstrong, that an honour in itself. But it was Al Bowlly who was besieged after the show by a mob of female autograph hunters.

This is how the *Melody Maker* in September 1933 reported Al's first solo variety performance:

'SENSATIONAL ACCOMPANIMENTS BY NEW PIANISTIC DIS-COVERY . . . On Monday night, 11 September 1933, full half an hour after the Holborn Empire had closed, there was an extraordinary scene in Holborn, when a mob of 100 or more people, mostly women, besieged Al Bowlly for his autograph, around a sand-bin on which he was perforce made to write his signatures. He had just enjoyed a personal triumph on the stage, where he appeared for the first time as a solo variety artist.

PIANIST PAR EXCELLENCE
Solo is perhaps the wrong word, as it would do less than justice to Al's brilliant accompanist, a young man from Singapore by the name of Monia Liter, a pianist of exceptional all-round ability. Liter comes from a poor family and is in many respects a self-taught musician. Not only does he play the piano with the ability of a concert virtuoso, but in some way or other he has acquired a rhythmic style seemingly every bit as futuristic as Fred Elizalde's. Some of his blue harmonies when he was accompanying Al were most arresting, and he certainly is an accompanist of no mean order. Al also gave him the opportunity of featuring a solo, when he played a most interesting transcription of *Please*. It is said that Liter is also a fine arranger, and it seems quite evident that we shall be hearing a great deal more about him in the near future.

A SIGH FOR THE BAND
Although Al had safeguarded himself satisfactorily in this matter, it cannot be said that no one missed the usual band support which he enjoys. It is indeed questionable whether any crooner can possibly be

as good without his usual orchestral accompaniment. Opening in a simple curtain set, Al introduced himself with *Some of These Days*, without the use of a mike. His voice and his deportment were easy, although he has yet to acquire the art of avoiding restless movements of the hands. He got into his stride with *Learn to Croon*, using one of the two mikes which was definitely superior to the other, and this number suited him down to the ground and produced a warm response from the audience. Monia Liter's delicate variations in the accompaniment, both on piano and celeste, were charming to a degree. The next number was *I Cover the Waterfront*, sung leaning against the proscenium arch and without the mike. This is a number in which Al always registers a tremendous amount of sentiment and those near enough to the stage could plainly detect real tears in his eyes! When he concluded his last chorus, this time with a very inferior mike, the reception could only be described as rousing.

THE NUMBERS

He followed this number with *Minnie the Moocher*, in which the usual band harmonies were definitely and sadly missed, notwithstanding the fact that Liter was as good as any two average pianists together.

After this came Liter's piano solo, and then Al again, singing *A Brivela der Mama*, alternately in Yiddish and English with the mike on. The next number was *If You Were the Only Girl in the World*, and it was here that the first real sign of inexperienced stagecraft showed itself, because, without looking at what he was doing, he put out his hand to seek the support of the piano and groped vainly for it as he was too far away. Nevertheless, the number provoked loud cheers and the first part of his signing-off tune, again *Some of These Days*, was drowned in the applause.

BEFORE THE TABS

So enthusiastic indeed was the audience that, after taking several bows, he was compelled to come before the tabs and sing yet another number, choosing *Brother, Can You Spare a Dime?* In this number many a lesser artist might have come a cropper, because, for some reason or other, he had slipped on an old ragged jacket of such peculiar Norfolk cut that it aroused a few titters in the auditorium. Nevertheless, these soon died down as he progressed into this number, which suits him so well, and he definitely held up the show at its conclusion. Making all allowances for his obvious anxiety to please on this his first solo variety date, there can be no question that Al has sung better, but he did enough to prove that he is a great draw and a real top-liner and, had he been better served with more efficient mikes, he would undoubtedly have sung to even greater effect.

He certainly has no peer among British crooners.'

At this time, Al's signature tune was *Some of These Days*, which many people will associate with Sophie Tucker, rather than Al, who also featured

Brother Can You Spare a Dime? as a speciality number which went down well with audiences because of the line *Say don't you remember, they called me Al, it was Al all the time.* In fact this song became associated with Al even more than *Some of These Days* and when he later returned from America, he adopted it as his theme tune.

Unfortunately, Al never made a solo recording of either of these songs, for reasons that are best known to him. It is unusual not to make a recording of one's signature tune, and Al did have, in the main, his own choice of material for his solo records. Al did sing a short chorus of *Brother Can You Spare a Dime?* on a 12-inch Lew Stone 78, a medley entitled 'Lew Stone Favourites'. However, Al did sing his *Brother* on the air in full and an air-check (recording of a broadcast) of this song has recently come to light. This apparently was recorded in America during 1938 over a short-wave radio. Despite fading and distortion, which one expects on short-wave radio, one is at least able to hear how Al put over his signature tune on a recording which has survived 3,000 miles and nearly 50 years.

By November 1933, the Lew Stone band, of which Al was still a member, changed its regular evening engagement from the Monseigneur Restaurant to the Café Anglais, and the success of the band and its vocalist continued to rise. Appearing on radio, record, stage and even the cinema screen as well as with the Lew Stone band, then reckoned by many to be Britain's best, it was true to say that Al had reached the top of his profession. He was earning a good salary and was able to afford to bring his mother to London from South Africa for a few months. This was the first time in ten years that he had seen a member of his family.

Al with his mother

February 1934 saw the Lew Stone band starting a successful series of one night stands for Mecca who, again, kept Britain's leading band and vocalist in the public eye. At the London Palladium Al was seen for the first time to use a hand-held microphone – something modern day singers take for granted. But in those days Al had not long previously been seen singing through a megaphone. Also, in 1934 the band moved its regular evening engagement back to the Monseigneur Restaurant where they remained until it was converted into a cinema in the summer of that year.

During 1934, Al won the distinction of being the first crooner to be given a solo spot on the BBC. It was a very proud moment when he stepped up and sang two hits of the day that he later recorded, *The Very Thought of You* and *True*. Pathé made a short film of his variety act in the same year in which he again sang *The Very Thought of You*, which was shown in between feature films at the cinema in a series known as Pathétone Weekly. The film has a humerous opening. Al is 'hustled' onto the film set against his will uttering protestations including 'I've got work to do!' He gives up his struggle eventually and says 'Folks, Pathé have got me at last! Now where is my piano player?' As Monia Liter is similarly 'hustled' on, Al sits on the grand piano, Monia commences to play, still wearing his trilby hat. Al takes the hat off Monia's head, hurls it across the room and commences to sing. The arrangement of the number is quite different to that on the gramophone record. The film was shot in a small studio in Film House in London's Wardour Street.

Al had a vitality and perennial freshness which was due to keeping fit and was lithe, muscular and bright-eyed. So keen on this was he that he now started taking boxing lessons from the ex-featherweight champion of Great Britain, Johnny Brown.

Around this time Henry Selmar and Co published a series of would-be teach yourself music books each bearing the name of a member of the Lew Stone band. For example, Nat Gonella on trumpet playing and Lew Stone on orchestrating. One of these was entitled 'Modern Style Singing (Crooning) by Al Bowlly', but it is believed that some or maybe all of this book was *ghosted* for him. Nevertheless the book is interesting and in it is discussed various aspects of singing from general aspects to breathing, tone production, vibrato etc. The book also explains, albeit briefly, how to read music and contains plenty of voice exercises that the budding crooner is strongly advised to practice!

The West End hotels would close around 2am and some nights after work was through, musicians would go to clubs such as the one called The Bag o' Nails. This was a place where musicians would go for a 'blow' and when Bowlly would visit, occasionally jazz pianist Gerry Moore would accompany him.

It is generally thought that in Al's period with the Lew Stone band, he had perfected his vocal style. This is indeed borne out by the many records he

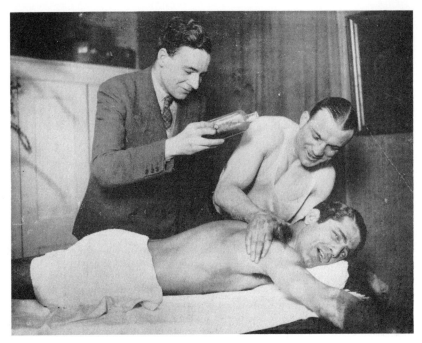

Above:
Al Bowlly, keen on physical culture, receives a massage

Above right:
A publicity shot of Al in the bath

Below:
Al Bowlly with Lew Stone and his Band

made, not only with Stone, but also those he continued to make with Ray Noble. Al's freelancing days in the recording studios were for the time being over, although he did make a few special appearances. One such occasion was in February 1933 when Al sat in with Jack Jackson's new orchestra and committed four titles to HMV's wax. In the post-war years Jack became very well known as a comedy disc-jockey, on BBC radio.

During this period, Al also carried on making solo records and for one of these, the Cole Porter classic *Night and Day*, the orchestral accompaniment was directed by no lesser person than Carroll Gibbons.

Even though Al was now at the peak of his career, he was always very friendly and kind to his fans even to the extent of inviting them to his flat or helping them out financially. He also gave encouragement to up-and-coming singers. One Al Bowlly enthusiast, Frank Haley, wrote telling of the time he met Al at the Holborn Empire. Frank told Al that he thought Al could sing better than Bing Crosby and he recalls that Al demurred saying that Crosby was highly talented. Frank continues:

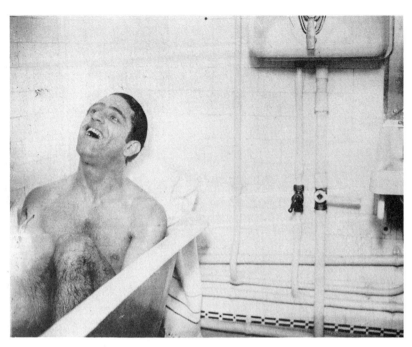

Jack Jackson, the bandleader who became a disc jockey. Al was Jack's first vocalist

'Al was not only a great personality – he was disarmingly modest. Al loved what he did, he was sociable, kind to people – certainly kind to me, a mere youth he need not have bothered with. Instead we chatted at length, we got on famously and he invited me to a party. I had a *Melody Maker* with me; it had a picture of Al at an organ grinder's machine and he autographed it for me. He said that he had spotted the poor old chap, stopped, sung and played to make money for him. Typical kindness of Al Bowlly.'

CHAPTER NINE

Top Hat
1934–35

During Al's spell with Lew Stone, he also appeared in a variety of radio programmes including 'Hear Hear' with Archie de Bear, 'Friends to Tea' and 'Crooner's Corner'. He also appeared in Eddie Pola's programme 'America Calling' which was a burlesque based on an American sponsored radio programme. A 12-inch 78 was issued on the Columbia label based on this programme with the same title and involving Al impersonating Bing Crosby under the name of 'Bang Horsby'.

Al also appeared on the radio with Ray Noble and had been recording continuously from late 1930 with Noble for the HMV company side-by-side with his Fox/Stone/solo records for Decca.

Earlier we recorded the meeting of Al and Ray Noble in 1930. Al was never credited with his work with Noble on the records, but reviewers in newspapers and magazines nearly always mentioned the vocalist's name. During the period of Al's association with Ray Noble he was featured vocalist on all the original recordings of Noble's compositions which have become standards in the evergreen song books. The three Noble songs *Goodnight Sweetheart, Love is the Sweetest Thing* and *The Very Thought of You* will always be remembered as Bowlly/Noble classics.

Except on rare occasions, the Noble band had no identity outside the recording studios as its musicians were all members of other bands. On one such exception the band made a rare public appearance at a Cambridge May Ball in 1933. Another occasion was when the band went to Holland for a summer season later that year. With Ray went many of Lew Stone's men including Al Bowlly to the Kurhaus at Schveningen. Al took with him 22-year-old Margaret Fairless, a really beautiful girl who was always known as Marjie. Like Freda, she had been a dance club hostess, but unlike Freda, she found approval with Al's fellow musicians. Marjie knew that other women flirted with Al – and that he responded – but she took it all in her stride. He didn't try to hide anything from her as he was an open book and to a certain extent had a simple approach to life. Strangely enough, no one now remembers anything about Marjie's background; however it is known that she came from Portland in Dorset. In Schveningen the band stayed at the Palace Hotel where they were treated as VIPs. Al and Marjie shared the

Max Goldberg and Freddy Gardner, famed instrumentalists who worked alongside Al with Ray Noble's Orchestra

honeymoon suite, as they were travelling as man and wife although Al was still legally married to Freda.

The engagement in Holland was very informal. Unlike places such as the Monseigneur Restaurant the band were allowed to fraternise with the patrons. They played for tea dances in the afternoon and in a large ballroom in the evening.

During Al's spell with Ray Noble at HMV he was hired solely as a vocalist, Bert Thomas doing most of the guitar work. However, according to the *Melody Maker* Al went to Holland as guitarist.

Ray Noble had the pick of any musicians in London and it was indeed a privilege for Al to have been the regular vocalist with the orchestra. During the period from 1930–34, Ray Noble's records were also issued overseas, especially in Europe, India, Australia and America and they proved to be very popular in these countries, particularly in the USA. This popularity led up to RCA Victor, the company issuing Ray's English recordings in America, convincing Noble to come to America to form an orchestra. The intention was for the orchestra not just to make records but also to appear before the American public. He accepted the offer to work in America, and arrangements were made by Ray with Rockwell–O'Keefe Inc, the American Artistes' Representatives. Ray Noble asked two of his English bandsmen to go with him, Al Bowlly and Bill Harty, the band's drummer. Bowlly gladly accepted the offer and viewed it as the break he had been looking for.

When the news broke that Al was leaving for America, a contemporary of his, Maurice Elwyn, wrote in the magazine *Rhythm* that he was sorry that Al was leaving Britain and blamed this on the British impresarios for not exploiting him. Part of the article reads as follows:

> 'Instead of being glad that Al Bowlly is going to America, I feel sorry about it, in fact it seems such a great pity to allow a potential box office colossus to slip through the fingers of British showmen. With a Scotchman's natural sense of values, I feel that when we lose Al Bowlly we have lost an excellent business opportunity. Although you may think Al is a star, I can safely say that he has never been correctly exploited in this country. He is regarded by the BBC as a "crooner" – the chap who sings with Lew Stone. But as an artist the BBC has done nothing in the joint interests of themselves and Al Bowlly. Most popular of all our crooners Al has never been given a real opportunity to show what he can do. Does the BBC know that he can sing? I doubt it. Not one of our "business" showmen has had the foresight to see big money in Al Bowlly as a ready-made star, already popular with millions of listeners, appealing and chock-full of personality. Here was Al, just waiting to be handled in the right manner for radio, stage and films, and nobody saw the opportunity of making real money until it was too late.

Al with friends on the beach

I say, most emphatically, that had I the capital I would never have let Al Bowlly go to America. I would have exploited him in England in every possible way and would have made money with him! Well directed in pictures, Bowlly would have been unsurpassed, for his general demeanour and appearance particularly qualify him for this type of work. When his fans meet him they are never disappointed – they are agreeably surprised. Al's great charm lies in his childlike sincerity. Although he might be a tough handful in an emergency, he always wants to be friends. He detests quarrels and is profusely affectionate with his pals. Although Bowlly is a dreamer, he is the kind of dreamer who makes his dreams come true and that is why he is going to America. It is true that England has recognised Al Bowlly, but he had to go to America to find stardom.'

A different opinion was held by Christopher Stone, a firm friend of Al's who will be remembered as being the world's first disc-jockey. He wrote as follows in the *Daily Express* of 29 August 1934:

'What will happen to Al Bowlly in America? He has a hankering for films and wants to prove that he cannot only croon with the Bingiest but box like Baer and dance like Fred Astaire. He looks gorgeous in plus fours that sweep the ground. But no doubt, now that Tommy Rockwell is exporting him to join Bing Crosby, the Boswell Sisters, the Mills

Al saying goodbye to two friends before leaving for America

Brothers and the rest of the harmony circus, he will find himself crooning to unknown millions.'

In the article Christopher Stone goes on to explain how he lost a cigarette case inscribed 'Recording an Unbreakable Friendship' which Al Bowlly had given to him. He comments:

> 'Now that he (Al) is gripping his pack – or is it packing his grip? – for the leap with Ray Noble and Bill Harty into the American dance world the loss of that cigarette case recording our unbreakable friendship seems more intolerable than ever.'

Which of these two different predictions was to be the more accurate? Al's trip to America was certainly one of the high spots of his career. But was he to achieve the stardom envisaged by Maurice Elwyn?

Al Bowlly handed in his notice to Lew Stone in mid-October and he sailed with Marjie from Plymouth to New York on the *Île de France*. A few months after their arrival, Al married Marjie on 18 December 1934, the third anniversary of his marriage to Freda, in Jersey City. Ray Noble and Bill Harty were witnesses, but they did not notice, or did not object, when Bowlly declared to the court official that he had not previously been married!

Al and Marjie had set themselves up in a modest hotel, the Abbey-

The lovely Eve Becke who duetted with Al on a Ray Noble disc

A holiday snapshot of Al and Marjie

Al with Ray Noble and a friend

Victoria near Broadway, residing there and taking their meals in restaurants.

Before they could get down to working in America, Messrs Noble, Bowlly and Harty had to solve two problems. Firstly they were not familiar with the New York music scene and did not know who the musicians were and how to hire them. The second problem was caused by the Musicians' Union who had to be convinced that the three Britons would not be taking work from the Americans, but on the contrary would create more jobs. The first problem was solved by the Rockwell–O'Keefe Agency who were managers to both Bowlly and Noble. They put Noble in contact with an arranger and trombonist who was experienced in the New York music scene and would be able to help the Britons. This was Glenn Miller, and he agreed to organise a band for Ray Noble.

While Miller was organising the band, Ray Noble went to Hollywood to write some songs for films. But before he went to California, he landed a 26-week contract to star in a series of radio programmes sponsored by Coty Cosmetics. This was to start as soon as the orchestra was ready. Meanwhile, Al Bowlly, whilst waiting for the formation of the orchestra, commenced recording with Victor Young and his Orchestra. Four tracks were recorded, two with Al as the principal artiste and two featuring Al as vocalist with the Orchestra. These recordings were a fine start to his career in America. Al also broadcast with Victor Young in a sponsored radio programme 'The Bromo–Seltzer Hour'.

Bill Harty, the drummer who went to the USA with Ray Noble and Al Bowlly

Al and Marjie setting off for the USA in 1934

One of the first things that made an impact on Al when he arrived in America was the high cost of living. He later wrote:

'Within ten days of our arrival I realised I was actually spending 60 dollars a week more than I was earning. I tried to cut things down – but at the end of the month I found myself £40 out. Life is like that in New York. The cost of living is higher than I've ever known it in any other place in the world. Everybody dresses smartly, lives smartly. It's all done on credit.'

The orchestra quickly took shape, and the Musicians' Union had apparently realised that Noble would be making jobs for American musicians rather than taking jobs from them. Glenn Miller soon got a really great band organised containing such notable stars as Charlie Spivak, Bud Freeman, Pee-Wee Irwin, Will Bradley and Claude Thornhill. Miller was to play trombone in the orchestra which was an outstanding unit containing many men who went on to front their own bands in later years. It was ready in January 1935, by which time Ray Noble had returned from Hollywood.

One of the first jobs for Noble was to direct an orchestra backing Al Bowlly in the Victor recording studios in New York, in January when Al went over to the top-flight HMV company for his solo recordings, which was the highest compliment that could be paid to a popular recording artiste in those days. His first HMV solo (recorded and issued by the associate company, Victor) was *Blue Moon* – a record considered by many to be Al's all time finest. This was one of four titles recorded at this session. It was the first record made in America bearing Ray Noble's name on the label but now the tables had turned. Unlike the credits on their English records, Al Bowlly was the principal artiste with Ray Noble only 'director of the accompanying orchestra'.

Radio in America, unlike in Britain at that time, was commercial. Al with the Ray Noble Orchestra was heard several times weekly not just in New York, but coast to coast. These were sponsored radio programmes, the best known being the already mentioned Coty programme. The transmissions were recorded on metal transcription discs – but they were for broadcasting use only – not for commercial issue. However, in 1975 several of these old transcription discs were traced and the contents transferred onto long-playing records. Therefore, 50 years on we are able to listen to the way the band sounded back in the 1930s to American radio audiences. These broadcasts being made available to the general public means we can hear Al singing many songs which he never recorded for commercial issue, including *Lullaby of Broadway, Solitude, In a Little Gypsy Tea Room* and *I'm Misunderstood.*

The Coty Hour was a weekly 30-minute programme broadcast every Wednesday evening on NBC's station WEAF, starring Ray with Al simply being introduced as the vocalist for the numbers that he sang, sharing the vocal work with the singing group The Freshmen.

The large American radio audiences responded overwhelmingly towards Al and he later recalled (with probable exaggeration):

> 'The first thing that amazed me was the terrific pull of radio in America. Rudy Vallee showed me the letters he received after one broadcast. It was not uncommon for him to receive as many as 75,000 pieces of fan mail following each broadcast. And in addition, a barrage of telephone calls from his admirers immediately following each programme. I was filled with envy when Rudy showed me his well-organised office that he maintained just to deal with his radio fans. But within ten days of opening at the Rainbow Room and broadcasting on network radio, I had the happy experience of seeing the same type of fan mail staff and phone operators frenziedly busy handling the incoming enquiries about the "new British singer".'

Al also appeared on the radio with other bands as a guest and in particular signed with NBC for 36 half-hour programmes with the Al Goodman Orchestra. One broadcast with Ray Noble was actually beamed back to England.

The Ray Noble Orchestra commenced recording for the Victor Company in February 1935, making Al's first title *Soon* in a line of 35 as 'featured vocalist' with this orchestra. Apart from recordings and broadcasts, the only work the orchestra had was some college one-night stands. Nevertheless, all this earned the band enough money to pay the bills.

In America, Al met some of his relatives including his cousin Alfred Ne-Jame who was a student in a college not far from New York City. Mr Ne-Jame recalls the times he spent with Al, his wife Marjie and Mr and Mrs Ray Noble:

'I can recall the several times Al took me under his wing during my junior and senior years at college whenever I had a week's vacation. He would finance my trip to New York City or to other cities where they were scheduled. He exposed me to the life of a popular vocalist and to those who surrounded Ray Noble and other musicians and entertainers. It was a new world to me and my cousin Al spent all kinds of time and money on me as if I were his brother or son! I lived in the best of hotels, enjoyed dining in the swank eating spots of New York and Boston and other big cities. I always accompanied Marjie and Gladys Noble while their husbands were on the bandstand. And what a time I enjoyed at the Rainbow Room, time and time again! I lived in a glamour world and it took years before I settled down to the real world around me.

I recall that I brought a carload of classmates from college to my hometown of North Adams when I knew that Al and Marjie were coming for a weekend visit. They were as motivated as I about the

Ray Noble with his American Orchestra

77

world of vocalists and entertainment. We got a group together and went out to the ball park where we played soccer and although my classmates and I were on the college varsity soccer team we were astounded at the speed and agility and expertise Al displayed on the field. We all wanted him to coach us – he was that good! He could outrun and outdistance all of us, and most of my group were first class athletes. The astounding part of it all was that Al must have been at least 15 years or more older than any of us!

He used to embrace my father, his uncle, and cry about describing his mother, father, brothers and sisters and comment on how he was going to send my father and mother to South Africa, Jo'burg or arrange for his mother to join my father. And he used to pick up my mother and swing her around as he embraced and kissed her. She was a short and small woman who could be easily picked up as he did. It was Christmas whenever he visited the family! And Marjie was a princess whom he adored.'

Alfred Ne-Jame recalls that Al displayed various family traits such as being clean, tidy, a smart dresser, warm hearted and hot tempered. He recalls that Al loved children, although he never had any of his own, and whilst Al was over-generous, if he discovered he was being taken for a ride he would become a different person with a blazing temper. Mish Bowlly confirms that he was excitable, but not violent. As Ray Noble said, everything to Al was either black or white, there were no in-betweens. Even if Al did lose his temper with someone, he would soon calm down and never bear any malice or hold a grudge.

For all this, Al had a magnetic personality and his cousin Alfred remembers than when Al walked into a room, everyone stopped talking and were compelled to just look at him! He got on well with people as a rule, especially with the students.

Above:
With a relation in the USA

CHAPTER TEN

My Melancholy Baby
1935–36

During the first few months the band was making a very good name for itself in New York and work prospects were very good. On 31 May 1935 the Ray Noble Orchestra opened at the exclusive Rainbow Room in the Rockefeller Centre, 65 floors above New York's Fifth Avenue. The band were instantly successful at this venue and they commenced broadcasts from there. The smart set who patronised the Rainbow Room were very impressed with the Noble band and the voice of star vocalist, Al Bowlly.

A short time after their appearance at the Rainbow Room, Ray Noble arranged with the Music Corporation of America for the orchestra to appear at other prominent night spots, including the elite Astor and New Yorker, plus the concert halls.

In 1935 the orchestra appeared in the film *Big Broadcast of 1936*, although Al did not have a solo spot in this. However, being on the set enabled Al to meet his one and only singing idol, Bing Crosby, who was the star of this film. Bing was the world's greatest crooner, according to Al; in fact on one occasion he bought some of Bing's records to give to a girl friend rather than his own. The girl in question agreed when Al expressed the view 'Bing can really sing'. Bing remembered his meeting with Al and he recalled in a post-war interview many years later that 'Al was sure a fine fellow'.

Although one American correspondent of mine would dispute the fact that Bowlly was sufficiently popular in the States to rival Bing Crosby, it is true that in one popularity poll in America in 1936 the top three places were as follows:

1 Kenny Sargent
2 Al Bowlly
3 Bing Crosby

Al was now riding high in America and his photograph even appeared on sheet music there publicising a song called *Every Minute of the Hour.*

Al later recalled three amusing anecdotes from his New York days, which may have been based on actual happenings.

On one occasion in question Al was in a desperate hurry getting changed at his hotel as he was already late and he broke his braces. He telephoned to

the hotel office asking for a new pair to be sent up urgently. Presently there was a knock at the door and upon opening it, Al found a carpenter holding a brace and bit. The carpenter said, 'Look here Mister, if you want anything doing to the furniture, you had better let me do it.' Al frantically explained that he wanted a pair of braces to hold his trousers up, only to be told that in America these are known as suspenders! Al's popularity in the States was such that he was mobbed as he arrived and left the Rainbow Room. One particular night he related in a press interview that arriving only a few minutes before he was due to go on, and not wanting to disappoint the army of autograph hunters he hurriedly signed a few books. Just as he was about to sign one of them he noticed the page was folded over at the top. He turned the page to see typed above the space where he would have signed, the words 'Please pay to the bearer on demand the sum of $8000'. It was addressed to Al's bank! Realising that he had been discovered, the crook who had tried on Al one of the oldest con-tricks to be tried on the famous, hurried off and lost himself in the crowd.

A favourite anecdote about Al being a staunch patriot happened one night in the States when he was in a theatre and the British National Anthem was played. Al stood to attention while the Anthem was being played, causing an American in the seat behind him to tug at Al's shoulder and irately tell him to sit down as he couldn't see the stage. As soon as the Anthem had been played, Al turned round and after one blow, the man who couldn't see the stage had to be carried out of the theatre. Although the foregoing may be just another fable, we do know that Al was patriotic. Having lost his previous British passport in 1933, he was issued with another one in June 1936 while he was in New York.

In a post-war interview about his New York days, Ray Noble had the following recollections about Al Bowlly:

> 'During the time I knew him, he fell victim to every pretty redhead, brunette or blonde. Although neither young or handsome, he exerted a fascination on the fair sex which I found almost frightening. Not that he was a cynical or sentimental Don Juan – he believed every romance while it lasted which might be 24 hours or a month. He was even a faithful letter writer for while and then forgot the girl's name.
>
> I wouldn't like you to think that Al was just a "ladies' man". Far from it: he was extremely masculine. Almost aggressively so. Competitive sport, for instance raised him to the highest pitch of excitement. Whenever we could in New York we dined at Jack Dempsey's Restaurant and then crossed the street to Madison Square Garden to see the ice hockey. Usually another fellow and myself would sit either side of Al to hold him down when the referee made a poor decision. Otherwise, he would be up, blue veins bulging out of his face, and starting to get out onto the ice to tear referee and players limb from limb.
>
> I remember at Dempsey's Restaurant one night, two drunks were causing a lot of trouble. Al was taking off his coat to take them both on when Jack Dempsey himself appeared looking very unlike a boxer in his black tie and dinner jacket, and restored peace with soft words and the mildest demeanour.'

His cousin Alfred Ne-Jame remembers that Al was very knowledgeable about sport and that he was an energetic person, 'Al walked so briskly that I had to run to keep up with him', and also recalls he did not read very much, being more interested in physical pursuits.

In August 1936 Al, with Ray Noble, returned to London for both a summer holiday and to fulfil some commitments. Originally it was hoped that the whole Rainbow Room Orchestra would be brought over to appear at the London Palladium. However, the Ministry of Labour refused a work permit for this.

The theatre critic of the *Daily Express* reported that Al was bitterly disappointed with England. Apparently, soon after he arrived home he was invited to appear in variety. According to the *Express* he asked for £250 a week but was offered only half that amount – the same salary as he was earning when he went away. Al said:

> 'I turned down the offer. It seemed ridiculous. I named a figure I am accustomed to earning. If it's too much money – all right, I don't want to work. I'm here on holiday. Funny thing is I still get about 400 letters a week from people in Britain. It makes one feel a little sad when home doesn't give one credit.'

Nevertheless, Al did work whilst on holiday making just one record and a short film. The record turned out to be the last Noble/Bowlly record made in England. It is now the collectors' item 'The Ray Noble Medley', a 12-inch HMV 78 featuring Ray Noble's compositions and on which Al sang *The Touch of Your Lips* and *Goodnight Sweetheart*. The latter number is perhaps the song most commonly associated with Al, and this version is perhaps his best rendition of it with a nice modern sounding accompaniment by the studio orchestra directed by Ray Noble.

The film in which Al appeared was another Pathé short, issued in the series Pathé Pictorial for showing between features in cinemas. In the film Al sings *My Melancholy Baby*, a song he once recorded as a solo during 1935 when he was in America, teaming up this time with Monia Liter for his piano accompaniment. The *Melancholy Baby* film opens with a shot of Al playing guitar in the Roy Fox band when the announcer introduces him as the singer who rose to fame with Fox and who subsequently was successful in America. The scene changes and Al comes on and introduces his song. Like the previous film in which he sang *The Very Thought of You*, this was also shot in Film House, Wardour Street, London. This film represented Al's last known appearance on the cinema screen.

The short break in England was soon over and Noble and Bowlly crossed the Atlantic again to continue their commitments in the United States. Ray Noble decided to take the band on tour and they appeared as far north as the Canadian border as well as in the Deep South. One press article reports that in Boston Al was attacked by a mob of female fans who tried to cut off locks of his hair as souvenirs, but this was probably another exaggeration or myth.

Al wrote on the reverse of the original 'Up at the Rainbow Room with financier Mr. Morris of New York, Anna Neagle, Ray Noble, producer Herbert Wilcox and myself'

The scene now changes to a city almost 8000 miles away – Johannesburg. Bowlly's younger brother Mish receives the following cable dated 10 November 1936, from his brother in New York City:

> Wire immediately if you have passport. If not, get one fast and be ready to leave London first week in December. Imperative. Depend on me for second class fare and expenses. Love to Mama & all. Signed Bootie.

Al had decided to leave America and return to England. The reasons why he made this decision have always been open to speculation. This varied from views that Al did not like the sophisticated American way of life to a statement that he got involved with gangsters and had to leave. Al refused to speak about his American experiences – it seemed to include bad memories for him. Because of this we may never know why he decided to leave for certain. But perhaps the following factors played a part. Firstly and simply he did prefer living in Britain which was the country he liked the best. He didn't particularly like the American way of life as is illustrated when a reporter asked him 'What do you want to do more than anything else?' Al's reply (not to be taken absolutely literally) was 'There's only one thing that I really want to do and that is to make enough money so that I can buy a 100-foot motor boat, go back to South Africa and go fishing.' Secondly, Ray Noble was offered a contract to join the Burns and Allen radio show which was broadcast from Hollywood. As the show already had a singer, there was no prospect for anything other than a minor part for Al. Thirdly, although he was not as ambitious as many entertainers, he was of the opinion that he could do better in England, especially as he now had the idea that he could get his own show on the road with his brother Mish. Alfred, Al's cousin said Al felt he was not getting the breaks in America that he deserved. For example, he was not happy with his billing as second to the band and although he was to appear in the film *Big Broadcast of 1936*, for some reason his contribution was edited out. (Perhaps it was felt that one popular singer, Bing Crosby who starred in the film was enough.) So at the end of 1936, Al Bowlly and Ray Noble parted company by mutual agreement.

It has often been said that the most typical sound of the Ray Noble Orchestra was that of the singing of Al Bowlly. This was true, for when Al left the band, it lost much of its identity and shortly afterwards broke up. Ray Noble recognised Al's vocal talent back in 1930 and it was through Ray that he made so many excellent records and was invited to America. With Al and Ray breaking up, what was surely one of the greatest dance music partnerships ended. Their last record together was made in New York in October 1936 and entitled *Where the Lazy River Goes By* and *There's Something in the Air*.

The musical press on both sides of the Atlantic vibrated with the news of Al leaving the Ray Noble Orchestra. Back in England the *Melody Maker* bore the headline AL BOWLLY LEAVING NOBLE AND RETURNING TO ENGLAND and went on:

'Cablegram advices from New York announce the startling news that Al Bowlly is severing all connection with Ray Noble and his Orchestra at the end of the year (1936) and is shortly returning to England. He is credited with the intention of coming to London to form his own band here, into which he is recruiting his brother, Mish Bowlly, who enjoys a high reputation in South Africa as a modern pianist and orchestrator.'

This short *Melody Maker* story concludes 'With Ray Noble in America, he was quite a success, but apparently not to such a degree that he does not think he can do better in this country.'

In America *Metronome* magazine of January 1937 carried the story, part of which reads as follows:

'Al Bowlly, earnest, genial, South African brunet, after years of association with Ray Noble and his orchestra, is leaving that organisation before it goes on its annual vaudeville tour, to return to England. Al was happy over here, but he claims that he has never been as happy as he used to be in Great Britain. Al has always been a tremendous favourite over there, and the set-up (he and his brother combining in the venture) of an Al Bowlly band has intrigued him so much, that he is forsaking more American fame and returning to England to recapture all of that which has been his over there.

Al's place in the Noble organisation is being taken by Howard Barry, who, as Howard Phillips, achieved much local fame with Leo Reisman some years back at the Hotel Brunswick in Boston, and who, since then, has been successfully singing out on the West Coast.'

In the same issue of *Metronome* was the following extract from their reporter in England:

'Michael (Mish) Bowlly, younger brother of Al Bowlly, is on his way here from his native South Africa to help his brother in the formation and direction of an English orchestra.

Al, whose work with Ray Noble has just terminated after a successful and lengthy stay in America, now returns to the country he likes best, and is determined, with the aid of Mish, to make himself even more popular in England as vocalist and conductor of this projected orchestra. Mish is, so Al has heard, a talented pianist and arranger; but Al will not know the actual extent of his brother's talent until they both get together in England, for they haven't met since 1920!'

It was not until he announced his departure from New York that Al realised how many friends he had made in the New York music world. Some of them got together and presented Al with a parting gift – a large leather suitcase with a silver plaque inscribed: 'To Al Bowlly from Abe Lyman and all the music men of New York City.' This indeed was a very appropriate tribute and gesture for Britain's favourite popular singer who had also won the hearts of the American public and music world.

Although Al was unhappy with his stay in America, looking back on it, it can be seen as one of the high spots of his life. Ray Noble later recalled that when Al was on tour in America he was leaving a trail of broken female hearts behind him, and was meeting Crosby and the rest of them on their home ground and beating them at their own game.

Whilst in America, Al sang many of the popular American songs of the day that have since become standards. Songs like *I've Got You Under My Skin*, *Easy to Love*, *Top Hat*, *Let Yourself Go* and *Let's Face the Music and Dance*. Many of these were, fortunately, committed to wax, but not all. One such number which Al sang but that will never be heard again by him was *Now I Lay Me Down to Weep*. It was written by Glenn Miller during his association with the Noble band. Al never even sang this number in public, but it was in later years to become one of the biggest song hits of the swing era when Miller re-named it *Moonlight Serenade* and adopted it as his signature tune.

All Al's records in America were pretty good, but one batch are worthy of special mention before we leave the American era of Al's life. They are of special interest because they were eventually issued on LP under a pseudonym. They were issued as 'Reginald Norman and his Orchestra with vocal refrain by Art Brady'. The orchestra was, of course, Ray Noble's as can be seen by the RN/AB initials. The titles were made, as far as can be ascertained, on a Western Electric Wide Range Vitaphone Recording for Associated Music Publishers Inc, New York, and they were originally made for commercial radio use. The titles included the following that Al never recorded commercially – *I'll Forsake All Others, You Were There* and *Under Your Spell.* On all these Al is in top form, although it is apparent that he had a cold, and are of better sound quality than any of the Ray Noble New York commercial records. The rendition of *I Can't Give You Anything But Love* is of particular interest as far as Al is concerned as his style on this is ahead of its time, containing improvisations of the kind which later became the hallmark of Frank Sinatra.

A publicity still from the film *The Big Broadcast of 1936*

CHAPTER ELEVEN

Brother Can You Spare a Dime?

1937

Al and Marjie Bowlly left New York aboard the *SS Berengaria* and arrived at Southampton on 16 January 1937.

Back in London the Bowllys moved into a flat at 23 William Mews, Knightsbridge. Al was soon to experience a certain amount of difficulty in re-establishing himself in this country. While in America, he faded from public attention in Britain as he had not been heard on the radio or seen on the stage for some considerable time. Nevertheless, many of the records he made with Ray Noble in the States were also issued over here and sold reasonably well to those who did remember him. These were the real dance band and crooner fans, rather than the general public.

Whilst Al was abroad, Sam Browne had become Britain's favourite singer, beating Al into second place in a *Melody Maker* poll later in 1937. The *Melody Maker* commented that 'he was a forgotten man'. This situation was not helped by the fact that at this time he did not have an agent. Lew Stone would certainly have employed him again if he had had an evening engagement in a restaurant or nightclub, but instead Lew was doing shows with the Hulberts.

Moreover, Al's voice was beginning to give trouble. He was soon back on the radio and guesting with Henry Hall with whom he broadcast *Take My Heart* and *Is It True What They Say About Dixie*.

However, Al's ambition was to get his own show on the road. In response to the telegram sent to Mish, Al's brother set sail to London on the liner *Balmoral*, his fare having been paid for by Al.

When they met it was for the first time in 14 years. Mish had never even heard Al sing. This was because Mish was only a child when Al left Johannesburg with Edgar Adeler and he had not been old enough to go out to the venues where Al used to sing. Mish moved into 23 William Mews with Marjie and Al.

Mish remembers the first time he did hear Al sing. Al, Marjie and Mish went to the Café de Paris where Al greeted a very distinguished looking couple. Mish asked Marjie who they were. 'They are Lord and Lady Mountbatten. They are great fans of Al's', came the reply. The manager then came over and said to Al, 'Welcome back – how beautiful to see you.'

The Café de Paris was very full but the manager was able to find them a table on the upstairs balcony. 'All of a sudden,' recalls Mish, 'a spotlight focussed on the upper balcony and pinpointed Al. He stood up and took applause and subsequently sang *I've Got You Under My Skin.*'

Just as Mish had not heard Al sing, Al had not heard his brother play the piano. But Mish was reputed to have become a good jazz pianist and when he played, Al was not disappointed.

Thus Al Bowlly formed his band which he called 'Al Bowlly's Radio City Rhythm Makers' who made their debut on 1 March 1937 at the Birmingham Empire, where they scored a resounding success.

The musical press at this time reported that Al received 200 telegrams of good wishes and predicted that the act would be No 1 attraction in vaudeville for a long time. The members of the band were: Mish Bowlly (piano); Percy Hampton (drums); Frank Baily (bass); Archie Slavin (guitar); Miff Ferrie (trombone); Teddy White (clarinet and baritone); Don Barrigo (tenor) and Bert Green (trumpet). Part of the *Melody Maker* report after opening night read:

> 'There is not a dull moment in the whole show, it goes with that easy swing which is the hallmark of a star, from the time that Al from behind the dropped curtain sings his signature tune *Buddy Can You Spare a Dime?* to his finishing number, the inevitable *Tiger.*
>
> Al could not have made a better choice, for there is enough talent there to make for the essential variety in such a presentation. Probably his best number is *Organ Grinders Swing* with some grand jamming by the boys, but the opening number *Everybody Jam* introducing each member of the band is excellent and novel. Al's medley including *Marta, The Very Thought of You* and *Spare a Dime* is his best solo effort. His show is himself in all his moods.'

This last sentence is indicative of the downfall of the Rhythm Makers. The whole act was centred around a vocalist with the band very much in the background. Other band acts of the time featured firstly the band, and the vocal was secondary.

Even after the band had made its debut, Al had ambitious plans to improve it by adding a personality girl singer and dancer. These ambitions were, however, never realised for the life of the band was to be cut short.

Shortly after the Birmingham debut, the band went to London where they appeared at the Paramount Theatre in Tottenham Court Road. They toured for several weeks playing in many well known places around the country including the famous Hammersmith Palais de Danse. They would also do a 'Ciné Variety' spot between feature films (sometimes appearing with other acts) at the more classy cinemas. One indeed got value for money in 1937. A good example of getting your money's worth reads in a report of a show they did at the Paramount. For 3s 6d. (i.e. 17½p) one saw two feature films, *Al Bowlly's Radio City Rhythm Makers* and several other acts. Despite subsequent events, Al's voice was reported as being first class on this night as he sang such numbers as *Chapel in the Moonlight, Organ Grinder's Swing, Marta, The Very Thought of You, Tiger Rag* and *Brother Can You Spare a Dime?*

The Rhythm Makers crossed the Irish Sea to appear in Dublin but on the first night there, Al's throat started troubling him and the next day he lost his voice. So for the rest of the week he had to apologise on the stage for being unable to do anything other than conduct the band.

The following week showed a gap in the engagement diary and the weeks ahead showed no better prospects of any work . . . so the inevitable happened and the band broke up. Dissatisfaction had been felt among the musicians who were generally relegated to fairly minor parts in the act and to quote *Melody Maker*:

> 'The moral was that even such a popular artiste as Al Bowlly could not run a stage band as a mere accompaniment unit in those days when jazz bands were expected to be a complete variety show in themselves. The sad story of Al Bowlly's Radio City Rhythm Makers is unfortunately summed up as seven weeks rehearsal for four weeks work.'

This cements the view that the venture was premature. A popular jazz instrumentalist such as Nat Gonella could run his own band, but the time had

Al Bowlly's Radio City Rhythm Makers rehearsing in 1937

not yet come in Britain for a show to be built around a singer. He was a band singer and never in a position to go round the publishers and choose his material. Many people tend to forget just that. Had he been living in today's profession he would have been a star in his own right.

It was generally felt that things were at a low ebb for Al. He had obviously under-estimated how short people's memories were when he came back from America. However, he now had an agent who dispelled these feelings in a forthright statement in the following terms:

> 'Al is topping the Paramount Variety bills at the following places for the next nine weeks and there are plenty more dates to follow: 5 April Blackpool; 12 April Manchester; 19 April Glasgow; 26 April Leeds; 3 May Liverpool; 17 May Newcastle; 24 May Old Kent Road; 31 May Brixton, and 7 June Cardiff. Everybody seems to have got hold of the wrong end of the stick. Al wanted a band against the best advice of the bookers and it was tried out for four weeks. Then the bookers confirmed their original contention that Al was better without a band and insisted on it going.
>
> No hardship was occasioned to the boys. They were all out of jobs when they were taken on and were told that there were only four weeks as a try out. During the rehearsal period they had full liberty to do session gigs and the like. We should know, as we frequently had to put off our rehearsals because of it.'

The *Melody Maker* headline in April 1937 was: A CRUSHING BLOW TO THE AMBITIONS OF AL BOWLLY. The Radio City Rhythm Makers were also a heavy financial loss for Al, who had very little business acumen – this fact also playing its part in the Rhythm Makers saga.

Al Bowlly's voice returned to him, he continued to tour the country, this time just with Mish on piano and Archie Slavin on guitar. On at least one occasion Robin Richmond accompanied Al on the organ. However, it wasn't long before Al's voice troubled him again and 'Indisposition' notices had to be posted where Al was due to appear.

It was around this time that Al's second marriage, to Marjie, broke up. They never divorced. This is confirmed not only by the absence of any documentation in the divorce Registry in London, but also by the fact that after Al died, Marjie's solicitor wrote to his solicitor in the terms 'We have been consulted by Mrs Margaret Bowlly, widow . . .' Marjie subsequently married Luigi Perella, the owner of a seafront club at Worthing in Sussex called 'Luigi's'. She died in Littlehampton on 22 July 1968 aged 57.

Mish Bowlly remembers Al introducing him to Helen Bevan, an attractive brunette. Al was to have a relationship with her that lasted until his final days. Helen, a Londoner, recalls that she was a teenager when she met Al at a theatrical party given by a mutual friend. She was an aspiring actress and show girl but as a standby had learnt the hairdressing trade. Later she became a hairdresser for shows and films. After they met they went out together for some months and then lived together.

Since his return from America, Al had so far made no records. It is unfortunate but we shall never be able to hear Al Bowlly's Radio City Rhythm Makers behind Al's voice. However, he did go back into the recording studios again in June to make a solo recording for HMV. This break in recordings represents the longest break in Al's recording career since his arrival in England.

The *Melody Maker* reviewed Al's one-week show at the Hammersmith Palais de Danse in July 1937 as follows:

> 'Repeated hearings of Al Bowlly's singing only tend to confirm the impression that as a vocalist he is unique, and his showing at the Hammersmith Palais, where he is appearing in cabaret with his new stage show proves this to the hilt, for despite the handicap of five weeks ill health, Al sounds fine.
>
> Apart from Al, however, mention must be made of the brilliant guitar playing of Archie Slavin to say nothing of Robin Richmond and his Hammond Organ, a scientific musical wonder which is worth going a long way to hear.'

The illness referred to above was throat trouble. Helen remembers that Al was out of his mind with worry as he thought that he had cancer. Although normally a virtual teetotaller, Al was now drinking port and brandy to soothe his throat.

It was at this time that Al and Mish met up with another of their relations, a dusky bandleader then working in London who was their second cousin. His name was Billy Gerhardi (real name Kerdachi) with whom Al made a broadcast.

In July 1937, shortly after a recording session with Ronnie Munro and his Orchestra, Al lost his voice once again. On the disc Al sounds as if he had a cold – but it was much more serious than this. His surgeon diagnosed a wart on his vocal chords and there was no one in England capable of performing the operation that was necessary. The only surgeon that could do this was in America, and he could only offer a 50–50 chance of success. Notwithstanding, Al decided to have the operation and the trip to America, and together with the medical fees it meant that he had to find a large sum of money. This was not easy so soon after his heavy deficit over the Rhythm Makers Band and subsequently being made redundant due to loss of voice.

Al had now reached what was probably the lowest ebb in his life. He was the sort of person who could be elated one day and in the depths of depression the next and was now the most depressed that he had ever been, for his voice meant everything to him. This had a very bad effect on his health and he lost over 30 pounds in weight. He later stated in an interview – 'The day came when I woke up and found my voice had gone. I

Three members of the Radio City Rhythm Makers, Al, brother Mish and Archie
Slavin. They went on tour together after the Rhythm Makers disbanded

stayed in bed. I cried and went on crying. I tried to force my voice – tried to
get out some sound, to swear at myself, to give vent somehow. I reckon I
knew how a woman would feel when she sees her child dying away. The
voice was gone – oh, but I can't begin to tell you how I felt. There aren't
enough words.'

Al Bowlly now made his last will and testament, leaving everything to his
mother in Johannesburg. He had no savings and he now had to find the
money for the trip back to America. Luckily, he had taken out an insurance
policy in 1932 and was able to use this as security to enable him to get an
overdraft from his bank. His bank manager let him overdraw up to £172. His
brother Mish also helped with funds and thus he was able to pay for the fare
and his medical bills.

This was really the start of a period of financial pressure for Al which was
to continue for the rest of his life. His bank account had always previously
been in credit: now he even had to stop sending the few pounds weekly to

Mish and Al in front of an advertisement for a provincial appearance

his mother in Jo'burg which he first started in 1932. Subsequently there was little money in his bank account which he rarely used.

In the summer of 1937 Al returned to the USA for the operation. Since his voice had gone, he had to turn down some very good offers. Just before he was to have the operation, he was offered a lucrative job to star in a stage show in Rio de Janeiro, Brazil, but he was no longer interested in the commercial prospects of organising another show. Soon after arriving in

America he entered hospital for the operation during which, it was reported afterwards, he had actually to sing to guide the surgeon's knife, since the slightest deviation could have ended Al Bowlly's career as a singer. Fortunately, the operation and a subsequent nasal one to free him from catarrh proved completely successful and Al became full of joy and thankfulness that he could sing again. Helen Bevan said that Al wrote to her every day from New York.

Being a deeply religious man, Bowlly believed that his voice was a gift from God. Biographer Sid Colin described him both as a 'devout Catholic' and a 'devout Christian'. The fact is that Al had faith and was a believer, but both Mish Bowlly and Helen Bevan say that he only attended church occasionally. Nevertheless Al regarded himself as Greek Orthodox. He took with him wherever he went a large silver crucifix which he wore round his neck and slept with under his pillow. He used to say that it would protect him and look after him. It didn't, but it illustrates his faith. Incidentally, he did not record any sacred songs, although he recorded most other types. Other singers of the day such as Sam Browne and Bing Crosby did, and it is a shame that Al never entered that field as he could have put over this kind of material so well with his intimate and sincere style of delivery.

Now that Al's voice had come back he was feeling on top of the world. Journalist Sidney Petty, after an interview, said that he had never seen a man so madly happy. Al had lost all his false friends and found one or two real ones who made up for everything. Al himself said:

> 'I've never been so happy, so cheerful, so contented of mind as I have been in these last seven months. I think right now, I'm the happiest man in the world, I've got something that I've been looking for all my life. Honest to God, in my own life – and I've had some good times – I've never been so happy.'

CHAPTER TWELVE

The Lonesome Trail Ain't Lonesome Anymore
1938–39

During the autumn of 1937, Al Bowlly had been through hell, but he came through it a wiser and happier man. Perhaps he believed, as many do nowadays, that his voice even improved as a result of the operation, becoming deeper and richer than it was hitherto.

There *is* a change of voice between Al's early recordings and his late ones, but there are other reasons that could account for this. Firstly, recording techniques were improving and therefore Al's voice tended to come over better. Secondly, Al was getting more experienced and his voice more mature as his career progressed. Thirdly, the style of number Al was singing was changing as the decade slipped by. If you are lucky enough to possess the records, compare some of Al's work before the operation *(Blue*

Maurice Winnick, the first bandleader to record Al in England after the singer's throat surgery

Sydney Lipton, one of the first bandleaders to approach Al upon his return from the USA

Rehearsing with Sydney Lipton and his Orchestra in 1938

Moon) with some afterwards *(I Can Dream, Can't I?)*, *Blue Moon* sounds more like Al after the operation and *I Can Dream* more like Al before! It seems just as likely that the change in the voice was due to the other reasons.

After the operation, Al didn't want to remain in America for long, although he did record there again. Indeed, as soon as his throat healed he was back in the recording studio again in New York with a studio orchestra billed as Al Bowlly and his Orchestra. When you listen to the six titles recorded, there is no doubt that his voice had returned.

Back in London in December 1937 he was eager to resume his work with renewed enthusiasm now that he had a *new* voice. The popular press gave good coverage to his return to England. Helen and Al moved into the Mapleton Hotel, which was near Ciro's night-spot. By this time Al's brother Mish had returned to South Africa.

It was not long before he was back in the recording studio vocalising with Maurice Winnick on Decca and soloing on HMV. However, the first bandleader to approach Al was Sydney Lipton. His first record with Lipton was entitled *The Lonesome Trail Ain't Lonesome Anymore*. Al was also with Lipton for his first broadcast since his return to England, which took place on 18 January 1938.

Bandleaders with whom
Al freelanced during 1938

Above left:
Lew Stone

Above right:
A young Mantovani

Left:
Felix Mendelssohn

Al and George Scott-Wood go over a number in readiness for an HMV recording session in 1938

Within a few weeks Al, having re-formed his association with Lew Stone, was soon back in the Decca Studios with this band. He also went into the Columbia Studios to record a couple of numbers with a conductor who was later to find world fame – Mantovani. Also at that time he attended a couple of sessions with Felix Mendelssohn, a descendant of the famous composer.

In an effort to re-establish himself, Al was determined to be the first crooner to make a record with just a backing group, no orchestra. He instructed his agent to find the best close harmony group to back Al on the record. He arranged for the Five Herons, a top-of-the-bill variety act to meet Al. They stipulated that they would not want their name to appear on the label or to receive royalties because they were an established act and did not know who Al Bowlly was! The record they made together coupled *Sweet as a Song* and *Sweet Someone*. It was made on 1 April 1938 with piano accompaniment by Violet Carson – later known for her portrayal of Ena Sharples on TVs *Coronation Street*.

Peter Heron, one of the Five Herons, remembers Al as a good looking man with crinkly hair. He was a very short, dark, powerfully built man having the shoulders and build of a Welsh miner and a firm handshake. The Herons were staggered by the amount of money Al was prepared to offer them and by his professionalism and dynamism. To illustrate a point Al would leap on to a chair or even a grand piano one handed and say 'Boys and girls what I want you to do is bring out that big sound there, just get the choir effect.' The Herons loved him for his warmth and enthusiasm. Peter Heron remembers Al always being very smartly dressed as if for a cocktail party and with a penchant for American ties. Although at that time a chain-smoker of Capstan Full Strength, his hands were always beautifully clean with manicured nails. He spoke about a pitch higher than he sung. His manner was charming and he had a great sense of humour although he did not tell jokes. He was invariably polite, never rude or vulgar. Despite his obvious charm, the Heron sisters found Al quite shy.

The Five Herons formed the opinion that Al made a lot of money in America although he refused to discuss his spell in that country. They recall that although he was generous he was careful not to waste his earnings. As a professional, Al knew exactly what he wanted to achieve but there was some evidence to suggest that he did not read music as he never looked directly at the arrangement when making alterations. Al always gave them the impression of being tremendously busy, arriving late for rehearsals, but no one knew how else he spent his spare time. However, Peter Heron recalls that he was well in with HMV and gave the impression of having plenty of money to live on whilst negotiating contracts. As regards Al's

Left: Al and a girl friend shunning publicity at Butlins Holiday Camp in 1938

Below: Bandleader Oscar Rabin who employed Al as vocalist for his Romany Band in 1938

100

voice, Peter Heron considered it would not have lasted many more years unless he was still recovering from his throat operation.

Today, the image remains with Peter Heron of a man who was generous, likeable, meticulous in planning, a perfectionist in execution and totally relaxed in front of the microphone – a true professional.

As well as freelancing in the record and radio studios, Al continued with his variety act, appearing up and down the country.

From this period Mish recalls that Al was earning good money – and spending it. 'He could have helped his family financially, but he didn't think. He used to lend money to people right, left and centre.' Al was a simple hearted, carefree person. His generosity was really foolishness and his attitude of living for the day did not help him when he needed money for his throat operation.

Al continued to record with Lew Stone throughout the year 1938 and these records equalled and some even surpassed the ones they made in the 1932–4 period. He also broadcast with Lew's band and continued to do so up to 1941, whereas their last records together were made in November 1938.

During the summer of 1938, Al appeared with this band at Billy Butlin's two new holiday camps at Clacton-on-Sea in Essex and Skegness in Lincolnshire. This is the first time that a top line band had appeared at Butlins. Apart from Lew Stone's band with Al, Butlin had lined up Mantovani, Gracie Fields and Vic Oliver, as well as sports stars including Horace Lindram and Joe Davis the snooker players. Al being a very good snooker player and Lew not being a bad one used to play them for the entertainment of the holidaymakers. The whole affair was very informal – the musicians forsaking their dinner jackets for maroon jerseys with white stripes. The band also made a broadcast from the camp at Clacton-on-Sea. Al was popular at Butlins, but in fact did not attract any more attention than other members of the band. This may be because Al was always seen with Helen Bevan and another girl friend who were staying at the camp with him. Also, it seemed that Al did not put himself out as much as the other musicians did for the campers.

In 1938 Al continued to make solo appearances and one report shows he appeared at East Ham Town Hall. However, this was not a come-down for him since other top liners appeared there, among them Denny Dennis. Although not a West End theatre, the microphone and reproduction system at this venue were of the highest order.

Another place at which Al was the first to appear around this time was the York Hall, Bethnal Green. The promoter of this show today remembers well paying Al what was then a fortune – £35 for his performance.

Around this time, a photograph of Al began to appear on the front of sheet music put on sale by the publishers. Some of the songs he lent his name to in this connection were *The Girl in the Alice Blue Gown*, *In My Little Red Book*, *So Little Time*, *Tears in My Heart* and *They Gave Him a Gun to Play*

Geraldo. Al sat in with Geraldo and his Orchestra for recordings during 1938 and 1939

With. These are all songs broadcast by Al, and the second mentioned was also recorded by Al as vocalist with the orchestras of Lew Stone and Mantovani.

Whereas sheet music with a cover picture of Bing Crosby, Sam Browne or Jack Payne, is fairly easy to find, music with Al's picture on is very difficult to come across for some reason. It tends to suggest that Al's photo did little to sell a song and perhaps explains why his photo only appears on a handful of sheets. And it confirms that Al still had not fully re-established himself in England and that he had not achieved the same degree of success since returning from the States as Sam Browne and Elsie Carlisle for example. However, Helen Bevan recalls that Al was trying to re-establish himself and that he had no doubt that he would succeed.

The world's first television service, provided by the BBC from Alexandra Palace in London, had been on the air since 1936. Al Bowlly made just one

With agent Leslie McDonnell

TV appearance during his lifetime. This was on 21 June 1938 in a 'live' broadcast from Harringay Boxing Arena. The fight was for the British and Empire heavyweight championship between Foord and Phillips. Al, being a very keen boxing enthusiast, having taken boxing lessons himself, was present. He was one of the celebrities at the ringside, also including George Formby and Jackie Crouch, all of whom appeared on the television outside broadcast chatting from the arena. Unfortunately, it appears that Al did not sing during the transmission.

In 1938 the famous Gaucho Tango Orchestra leader, Geraldo, formed a new band to play a wider and sweeter variety of music. Geraldo realised how popular Al was and asked him to sit in on the recording sessions for the new band, which Al agreed to do. He thus recorded with Geraldo from September 1938 to April 1939 during which time they cut 29 titles. On each of these Al sounds completely at home with the band, and many collectors agree that these are among his best band recordings, certainly of those he made since his return from America. Al appeared with the Geraldo band on record and also broadcast with him on radio although Al was never a regular member of the orchestra.

On 13 October 1938 a headline in the *Daily Express* read: CROONER'S EX-WIFE PAWNED JEWELS TO GET DRUGS. The article reports that

Al's ex-wife, Freda, was fined £10 for being in possession of Indian hemp. In the article, the figure of £250 is mentioned as Al's weekly earnings. But the article serves also to illustrate how faulty press information can be as it was several years out in stating Freda's age and the date she married Al. The headline serves also to show that Al was in the public eye once again and the whole report seems slanted towards it concerning a singer's ex-wife.

Before leaving 1938, a brief look at some of Al's radio appearances during this late 1930s period is worthwhile. On the BBC, Al could be heard both as a solo artiste and also singing with dance bands such as Lew Stone, Henry Hall (as a guest in his famous Guest Night programme) and Ambrose. These last two were of particular interest as Al never recorded with these bands, although Al had previously sung with Henry Hall and the BBC Dance Orchestra on one occasion in place of the regular vocalist Les Allen who was indisposed.

Al Bowlly could be heard also on the continental commercial stations that were beaming sponsored radio programmes from the continent to Britain. On Radio Lyons he was heard Sunday and Tuesday nights, on the programmes sponsored by Hinds Honey and Almond Cream, which he opened with the number *I Kiss Your Hand, Madame*. One of the most successful programmes for Al was on Radio Luxembourg and broadcast Sunday afternoon at 3.45, sponsored by Black Magic Chocolates. The programme

Advertising a Decca radio

Al at the microphone with Marjorie Stedeford

presented 'Music in the new sweet manner' with Monia Liter directing the Ace of Hearts Orchestra. Al was introduced as 'your singer of romantic songs'. A private recording still exists of this orchestra featuring the voice of Al Bowlly in which he sings *Pennies from Heaven* and *Shoe Shine Boy*. In both of these Al came over very well.

Also on Luxembourg, on Sundays, Al Bowlly was featured regularly in the programme Symingtons Sunday Night Excursion with Arthur Askey, Richard Murdock and Marjorie Stedeford, together with an excellent band directed by Harry Carr. Al often starred on Radio Eirann's popular evening programme 'Ten Minutes With a Star' as well as various variety shows on Post Parisien.

1939 was not a very good year for Al and he was not in the highest of spirits. Even his enthusiasm for work was flagging for Ronnie Munro, who provided the backing orchestra for Al's solo records for HMV, recalls that Al was always late for these sessions, as a contrast to the punctuality he was noted for in the early 1930s.

Freelance work was scarce for Al as far as records were concerned; only bandleaders Geraldo, Bram Martin and Reginald Williams used his services. Reginald Williams and his Futurists was a competent little outfit who were very popular in the West of England as Reg was Somerset born. Despite the fact the band had made many BBC broadcasts, they were not really nationally known. In 1939, Reg 'phoned Al Bowlly at his London flat and asked him to join his band at Bristol. With broadcasts and a summer season at Weston-Super-Mare ahead, Al took up this offer. Playing in the band at this time were such notables as Frank Weir, Felix King, George Chisholm and George Shearing. Earlier in the year Al had cut three recordings for Reg Williams for the Columbia label and these original 78s have become about the rarest of all those he made in England.

After the summer season, Al went back to making personal appearances up and down the country and these were successful as Al still had pulling power. Popular vocalist and instrumentalist of the day, Chips Chippendale recalled the time in the late 1930s when he worked with Al:

> 'It was about 1938 at a Sunday concert in Southsea when I was Sydney Lipton's vocalist. Al was due to appear with us as a guest singer and as it happened one of the titles turned out to be a number I had come to regard as my own. You know the sort of thing – *Goodnight Sweetheart* belonged to Al, *Body and Soul* belonged to Sam Browne, and so on. Just before the show commenced I was at one side of the stage trying to make my point to Syd about this tune being mine. After a few minutes of somewhat heated discussion, Al from the other side of the stage called out loudly with a big grin "So who's to perform this number – me or Caruso over there!" '

Rehearsing for a Radio Luxembourg show with Arthur Askey, Richard 'Stinker' Murdoch and Marjorie Stedeford

There was, however, not much work for Al at this time; he had to take whatever jobs were offered, however unsuitable they may have been. For example at Poplar Town Hall he is reputed to have been booed off the stage by moronic youngsters, although similar treatment had been handed out to other well known singers who appeared at that establishment.

Joe Gold, who ran a small band in the East End of London in the late 1930s remembers when his path crossed with that of Al Bowlly:

> 'I was at the time running a semi-pro outfit and we played local gigs around East London, mostly minor events such as Church Halls or Baths. We did however get a good gig at the Stepney Baths and Al had been contacted and agreed to come along and judge a crooning competition during the dance.
>
> When he arrived complete with a couple of friends he was immediately the target for all the local girls and he seemed to be in his element charming them with compliments and asides. He gave the first prize to a very attractive looking girl and I am sure that he was interested in a lot more than her vocal talents because whilst he was signing photos of himself and giving them to the other contestants he told this gal that he wasn't bothering to give her his autograph and gave her his telephone number instead with explicit instructions when and why she should give him a ring.
>
> A punch line to this tale is that he eventually disappeared down the spiral staircase at the back of the stage waving goodbye to all and sundry, but after about ten minutes whilst we had started up a number he re-appeared looking no longer charming and smiling but in a bit of a temper because, on leaving and collecting his overcoat and scarf he had taken a scruffy off-white one instead of his own white silk evening scarf and he thought it had been exchanged deliberately and was not amused nor could he be convinced that it had been a pure mistake. In fairness I must say that he was on a tight schedule and having to come back had put him behind in his timetable. However, I was able to get a smile out of him before he finally departed so we were left with fond memories of Al after all.'

Memories from Joe Gold serve to confirm the views about Al expressed by others who knew him, that he was generous and always had time for an attractive girl. Indeed Helen Bevan was experiencing the same old Al Bowlly that Marjie had done previously. Helen well remembers suspecting that Al had a string of casual affairs during their relationship as she didn't go everywhere with him, she was basically independent and following her own career. However, she does remember that Al's legal wife Marjie kept telephoning him to ask for money.

In 1939 Al became worried about his voice once again and in June of that year he suffered a severe throat infection which prevented him from overworking his voice. On the record he made at the time with Bram Martin

Left:
Bandleader Bram
Martin who employed
Al as vocalist with his
Band for a recording
session in 1939

Below:
Appearing with a
group of local
musicians at a Carnival
Dance in the North-
East of England in
1939
Frank Wappat

and his Band Al sounds a little like he did on the Ronnie Munro record that he made before his voice gave out in 1937. Although he did not require surgery on this occasion, his voice started to deteriorate and to some people it had lost much of its sparkle. He was still able to put a song over with all the feeling and professionalism for which he had always been noted, although it is noticeable from subsequent recordings that the power and range of Al's voice was beginning to diminish.

As soon as his throat infection had healed, he was able to fulfil a promise he had made to record the four winning entries in a song writing competition organised by *Rhythm* magazine. To quote from the July 1939 issue of *Rhythm*: 'With Claude Bampton acting as his accompanist he (Bowlly) laboured for six consecutive hours to wax the four titles and nobody could have been more meticulously careful about his work than this wonderful artiste. He was particularly enthusiastic about *Torn Sales* and *Dreamy Serenade*.' The two other songs recorded were *Just an Ugly Duckling* and *Champagne Waltz*. The pressings were not for commercial issue (although *Torn Sales* has since been issued on LP) but were to be given to the winners of the competition.

During the summer, Helen had been working abroad for a couple of months in San Remo where she was with a show. When she returned, World War II had broken out. Helen and Al moved into her mother's flat in Kensington, London where they occupied the basement. Helen remembers that Al and her mother got on well together. They stayed there for some while, but as Al was earning good money they were able to start renting a furnished flat in Piccadilly, Dukes Court, No 32 Duke Street. The building still stands to this day on the corner of Duke Street and Jermyn Street.

Now that the war had started it seemed to be the beginning of the end of the dance band era in Britain. Bandsmen were being called up and the dance bands were no longer the big attraction they were. Al Bowlly was now not getting the amount of work he would have liked. He had not been called up for military service since he was too old. He was to spend the early part of the war entertaining the war workers and blitz-weary population of London and elsewhere.

Bowlly had maintained his interest in sport and early in September he appeared in the very first Army Boxing show which took place in the South of England. Described in the *Daily Express* as 'the radio crooner', Al was reported as having led the boys in community singing after the boxing show. Al was also interested in swimming as this letter from a man who knew him in 1940, Mr Harold Franklin confirms:

'I had the pleasure of meeting Al for the first time during the summer of 1940 at Roehampton Swimming Pool (London) and we met there on a couple of weekends afterwards. He was a very good swimmer, but I asked him why he wore a swimming cap when he swam. He said it was

Relaxing with Helen Bevan and friend

to prevent the chlorine in the water spoiling his hair, of which he took great care. I could appreciate his point, as he had a jolly good head of thick black hair.

After I became friendly with him at the pool later on, I complimented him on his fitness and physique (as I myself was a keen gymnast and physical culture expert at the time). He asked how old I thought he was and I looked carefully and replied "about 35". He said "No, thanks for the compliment, but I'm 40." He certainly didn't look it.'

CHAPTER THIRTEEN

When That Man is Dead and Gone

1940–41

Al Bowlly had become very friendly with fellow singer and guitarist Jimmy Mesene as they were both of Greek extraction and in 1940 Al was best man at Mesene's wedding.

Both Al and Jimmy had been feeling the pinch work-wise. As mentioned earlier, there was very little session work available and they could not find good musicians available for accompaniment. And so the two of them decided to team up and form a double act. Mesene was a very competent guitarist and they would not have to rely on anyone else for accompaniment. The act was known as The Radio Stars with Two Guitars, and their debut was at the Theatre Royal, Newcastle-upon-Tyne in January 1940. Mesene's voice did not blend particularly well with Al's, which could not properly be partnered with any other male voice. It is now generally felt that this was the beginning of the end for Al.

The musical press argued at the time that this could be a top line act, but at the beginning, although vocally they were good, they still needed improved stagecraft. They were said to be too static and that on occasions Mesene saved the act from becoming slightly boring. Also the orchestral accompaniments and lighting were criticised for not being sufficiently dramatic.

The Radio Stars with Two Guitars was not, unfortunately, a top-of-the-bill variety act, although it was Al's bread and butter. After hours, Al kept on working as a soloist and broadcasting with Lew Stone and one or two others and singing in programmes such as 'Ack-Ack, Beer, Beer', a forces pro-gramme.

In May 1940, the Lew Stone band made its last stage appearance with Al Bowlly when it appeared at the Colston Hall, Bristol. The *Western Daily Press* commented on Al's performance as follows:

> 'The outstanding vocalist was, of course, Al Bowlly who has been right at the top of his profession for the past ten years or so. His per-formance showed that he has lost none of his skill and popularity and it showed, too, that he is more than just an excellent crooner – he is an artiste. He sang the poignant *Brother Can You Spare a Dime?* brilliantly. The audience would have liked to have heard more of him at the expense of perhaps Buddy Logan.'

Despite the fact that the power and range of his voice had diminished over the last year or so, obviously it was not considered detrimental to the overall performance. Al still had his style, could still inject his whole personality into his song and these are two important qualities that have made him the experts' choice over the years. However, he was by now singing in keys lower than copy key and his voice, was, unfortunately, little more than a whisper.

Al Bowlly was no longer Britain's leading vocalist for Joe Loss' singer Chick Henderson was now in the No 1 position. With all these problems, as well as the war, Al was not nearly as happy as he had been a year or two before. Nevertheless, Al and Jimmy were doing their part in entertaining the troops and war workers up and down the country.

On 19 May 1940, Al appeared in an all-star variety show at the Connaught Theatre, Worthing which was held in aid of Worthing Hospital. Part of the show was broadcast. It is interesting to note that both in the printed programme for the show and subsequent press reports, Al's name was incorrectly spelt, which perhaps gives credence to the fact that his star had by then been on the wane.

The recordings he made in May 1940 with Macari and his Orchestra were the last he ever made with a dance orchestra, but they were never issued. In July 1940 Al and Jimmy entered the recording studios to make the first record of their double act. They went on to record a total of four during the act's 16-month life.

Finally in 1940, Al Bowlly was interviewed by *Melody Maker* and the answers to the questions are numerical. The following questions and answers are reprinted from the issue dated 7 September 1940:

How old were you when you started singing?	6
When were you lead choir boy in South Africa?	12
When did you start crooning?	16
How many countries have you visited?	19
When did you join Lew Stone?	1932
When did you go to America?	1935
About how many miles have you travelled?	75,000
How many suits have you?	15
How many records have you made?	About 1000
How many favourite vocalists have you	1*
How many ties have you got?	60
How many cars have you had?	24
How many cigarettes do you smoke a day?	30

*Bing Crosby

How many haircuts do you have in a year?	14
How many clubs do you belong to?	0
How many teeth?	23
How many instruments can you play?	7
What is your biggest break at snooker?	67
What is your best score with three darts?	136
When you were a sprinter what was your best time for the 100 yards?	10.2
What is your height?	5' 7¾"
What is your weight?	11.2
How many pairs of braces?	12
How many shaves a week?	3
How many real friends?	4

I do not believe the above questions and answers should be taken seriously. There are inaccuracies: for example, he went to America in 1934 and the question 'how many shaves a week?' should have been 'how many shaves a day?', if the answer is three. The questions about weight and height appear accurate though.

A drawing of Ken 'Snakehips' Johnson who died in the Café de Paris disaster in 1941. Al and Ken made a jazz record of two Shakespearian sonnets

The year is now 1941 and a particular fan, Mrs Lucy Motley, who now lives at Southend-on-Sea, remembers when Al entertained her at the Poplar Baths at a time when London was being bombed nightly:

> 'Being great fans of Al my friend and I went to the Poplar Baths. Al was great. As we were trying to get to the stage when Al was singing he saw us come down the steps and called us to sit with him while he sang *Who's Taking You Home Tonight* and *Goodnight Sweetheart*. We were both on a cloud. Al stayed for a while and we talked about dancing, the bands, the war etc. I'll never forget that night – even though I have met many of the top bands our meeting with Al was the tops.'

Al Bowlly was a personal friend of coloured bandleader Ken 'Snakehips' Johnson; not only did they record together, but he sang with the Johnson band at their resident engagement at the Café de Paris in Coventry Street. The titles that Al had recorded with Johnson were jazz arrangements of two of Shakespeare's lyrics, *Blow, Blow, Thou Winter Wind* and *It Was a Lover and His Lass*, scored by the well known arranger of the period, Arthur Young.

Certain theatrical people considered it extremely unlucky to perform Shakespeare in this way and this record did turn out to be a bad omen for what followed. A tragedy in the music world occurred on 8 March 1941 when a bomb destroyed the Café de Paris and Ken Johnson was among the 34 people killed there. Al was naturally very upset when he heard the news, not only because he had lost a good friend, but, also because he now had a premonition that his own passing was soon to come.

During the early months of 1941, Al continued to do variety work in the provinces. Let Jack Whitfield, journalist in Scunthorpe from the early 1930s to 1950 take up the story (with acknowledgements to the *Scunthorpe Target*):

> 'I had a date with Bowlly at the Theatre on the Monday morning after the Cafe de Paris raid. I met him previously when he sung at the Scunthorpe Palais de Danse. He was a man easy to like – extrovert, generous, happy. That morning I found him distraught. Without a word he handed me a letter on blue paper in a woman's handwriting.
>
> "Al darling," it said. "Do be careful. I dreamt last night that you were standing with a black man and you were both blown away . . ." The letter was posted in the capital the day before the raid. "When I'm free, I sing at the Cafe," he said weakly. "If I'd been in London on Saturday, I'd have been standing with Ken."
>
> I reassured him the best I could. Pure coincidence I murmured. He would have none of it. He was (his words) a Greek and superstitious. He recovered to complete his week's theatre show, and the last time I saw him in Scunthorpe's High Street – my question "How's life now,

The Radio Stars with Two Guitars together with pianist Pat Dodd. This photo was taken during rehearsals for Al's final recording session *EMI*

Al?" brought the cheery reply so familiar to his friends, "Thank God, it's terrific."'

Incidentally, the charred remains of three of Al's music folders containing his name in gold lettering were recovered from the bombed nightclub and are held today as mementos.

Al carried on working and on 2 April 1941 he and Jimmy Mesene stepped into the recording studios to record two more songs. It was during the previous month that Al received the letter asking The Radio Stars with Two Guitars to make another record at the HMV studios at St John's Wood. HMV wanted a recording made of the Irving Berlin song *When That Man is Dead and Gone*, referring of course to Adolf Hitler. For the other side Al and Jimmy had their choice and decided upon *Nicky the Greek*. The arranger and accompanist for the session was Pat Dodd who turned up for the recording in his RAF uniform. The official HMV supplement photographer also turned up and took some photographs of the boys at work. These reveal that Al was tired and needing a shave. He was clad only in shirt and trousers with his tie slackened and top shirt button undone.

After the recording session Al and Jimmy carried on working in the provinces. They were booked for one week to do 'Ciné Variety' at the Rex Theatre at High Wycombe. At this venue they were top of the bill and because the accompanying organist was new, Al told him to stop playing as he was killing the act.

On the night of 16 April, a Wednesday, Al attended a small party after appearing at the Rex, at which he was the only one to remain sober. Al decided that he wanted to catch the last train back to London so that he could see a throat specialist as he had been worrying about his voice.

There are a few stories that, because Al narrowly missed being killed by a bomb a few weeks earlier, he consequently believed he had a charmed life and that he would remain safe. However, Jimmy Mesene later told the *Melody Maker* that before catching the last train from High Wycombe he said to him 'If anything happens to me, remember the Greek spirit'. So Bowlly returned to his flat in Dukes Court.

That night London was suffering one of the heaviest air raids of the war. Nevertheless, Al decided, as many did, not to bother to go to the safety of an air raid shelter. Helen Bevan remembers that Al was blasé in this respect and frequently did not go to the shelter. On this particular night, Helen went down to the shelter and left Al alone in bed with a cowboy book.

It was now the early hours of Thursday morning and the air raid continued. Al was still in bed when a land mine came silently down outside Dukes Court. As soon as the 'all clear' was sounded the hall porter hurried round to make sure all his tenants were safe. But on entering Al's room he found him dead on the floor by the side of the bed, evidently killed outright by the blast from the landmine.

Al Bowlly had died in the early hours of 17 April 1941. His death certificate described Al as a 'professional singer', misspelt his second name and gave the cause of death as 'due to war operations'.

Since Al had been killed in the early morning, it was too late for the news to appear in newspapers of Thursday 17 April, and instead the reports appeared on the next day. Most of the tabloids covered Al's death, although since the news was by now quite old, and Al was only one among many victims of the almost continuous air raids, the coverage was minimal.

Daily Express, Friday 18 April 1941, covering the heavy blitz of the previous night:

> 'The British official statement says casualties were heavy and damage considerable. Victims included: Lord Stamp, his wife and heir. Flying officer Lord Auckland. Al Bowlly the crooner.
>
> Lord Auckland and Al Bowlly occupied rooms in the same block of flats, in a third room between them was Judge Gerald de la Pryme Hargreaves. All three went to bed while the blitz was on. Lord Auckland switched on his light to read a book; Al Bowlly did the same. The Judge tried to go to sleep. Suddenly the building shuddered. Brickwork, plaster and glass flew everywhere. The hall porter hurried around to find his 40 tenants. On the second floor he went to the three adjoining flats, Lord Auckland was lying in bed – dead. He found Judge Hargreaves with a bad wound in the back of his head and sent him to hospital. Al Bowlly was dead. Lord Auckland, sixth baron and grandson

of a Viceroy of India was 46. He had been working at the Air Ministry. Al Bowlly, a South African, who crooned with Lew Stone's band had just returned to London from broadcasting engagements in the West of England.'

Most of the press gave an account of the incident. The *Daily Sketch* included on 18 April: 'Al Bowlly, the well known coloured singer was also victim.' (Note that this paper referred to Al as a coloured singer.) The music press, of course, gave greater coverage to Al's death, together with a tribute. However, when the news of the incident reached the *Melody Maker* office, the week's issue had already been printed in readiness for issue on the next day. Therefore the news and tribute appeared in the following issue dated Friday 25 April. This is how the *Melody Maker* brought the news of Al's death to its readers. (Front page headline):

AL BOWLLY PASSES

'Tomorrow, Saturday 26 at 10.30am Al Bowlly, killed in London's heaviest air raid last week, goes to his last resting place at the Westminster City Council Cemetery, Uxbridge Road, Hanwell. He is the second jazz celebrity to fall a victim to the German murder gang, and it is tragic that the first, Ken Johnson, was one of his greatest personal friends. For the benefit of friends and admirers who wish to pay tribute to his memory, there is a good train service from Paddington, or alternatively from Oxford Circus by Green Line, and No 17 bus. Al had been top-lining with tremendous success all over the country in vaudeville with Jimmy Mesene, who is carrying on alone, and will appear at the Empire Theatre, Glasgow, for the week commencing on Monday.

(An appreciation of Al Bowlly by Stanley Nelson appears on Page 4 of *Melody Maker.*)'

The appreciation ran:

SAY DON'T YOU REMEMBER, THEY CALLED ME AL . . .
'An appreciation of one of the Brightest Figures in British Jazz-singing History . . . by Stanley Nelson.

The above lines, from his famous signature-tune, *Buddy Can You Spare a Dime?* might well be the epitaph of one of the finest singers British jazz has ever known, and whenever they are heard in the future they will always recall a lithe, muscular, bright eyed figure "selling" his songs in a way that has never been excelled and rarely equalled by a Britisher.

I have watched Al Bowlly's career ever since he came here from Germany in 1928 as vocalist and banjoist to join Fred Elizalde's Band at the Savoy Hotel.

I have seen him rise from obscurity to international fame and when I met him last, only a few days before he was to lose his life in the latest

Luftwaffe murder raid on London, it was forcibly brought home to me just how unaffected and natural he had remained all through the years.

I thought then that he seemed troubled inwardly, under the bright optimism which flowed from him, and now I know that his hypersensitive, emotional nature had received a shock which all his laughs couldn't hide.

PROPHETIC LETTER

While he was playing a theatre date in the Midlands a week or two ago, he received a letter from someone who told him that she had dreamed that she had seen him talking to a Negro, and suddenly he had been blown to pieces!

Possibly the more solid and unemotional of us would have dismissed this, but Al was of a superstitious nature, and was plainly worried; all the more, because the very morning he received the letter, he also heard that one of his closest friends, Ken Johnson, had been killed.

He confessed to the MM Scunthorpe representative, Jack Whitfield, with whom he was on terms of intimate friendship that he believed that it was a warning to him. He freely admitted that the remarkable coincidence worried him. It was some time after this when I met Al in Denmark Street, but he hadn't rid himself of this fear and the third and concluding link in this appalling chain of circumstances has now been completed.

Al would have wanted to leave behind him a reputation not merely as a great jazz singer, but also as a man. I can say now that he was considerably older than most people suspected, and that only his remarkable enthusiasm for physical well-being and rigid adherence to exercise gave him a virility and a perennial freshness which belied his long experience in the business.

The homage of everyone with the welfare of the British jazz at heart must go out to this South African of Greek descent, who rode to world fame with those great recordings which Ray Noble made with the New Mayfair Orchestra. Those discs forced the attention of America to Britain's jazz and culminated in Al going to the States with Ray Noble and Bill Harty.

DOUBLE ACT

Although he was a terrific success in America, Al didn't care for the life there and he eventually returned home where the legions of fans who had listened rapturously to his singing with the great Lew Stone Band at the Monseigneur Restaurant soon had the opportunity to hear him in the flesh. For some years Al toured all over the country as a single act, but recently he had been for some time in partnership with Jimmy Mesene, and this had become one of the biggest vocal acts in variety.

Al and Jimmy were appearing at the Rex Theatre, High Wycombe last week and Al came back to his West End flat and went to bed during London's worst blitz. Reading in bed, he was killed – tragically enough not by a direct hit on his house, but by the blast from a bomb which demolished much of the street a few yards away.

There were many good judges, and the late "MM" cameraman Jack Butterworth was one of them, who considered Al Bowlly the greatest rhythm singer this country has ever had.

Concentrating as he did in late years on variety work, present day swing fans probably only knew him as a singer of pop songs. But to older fans, his pioneer singing with Elizalde, Lew Stone, Syd Lipton and other leaders will always be one of the brightest features in the small British constellation which had a very real place in the world firmament of jazz.

We in the *Melody Maker* office first learned of Al's tragic end late on Thursday afternoon, when a Press Association "flash" brought the news over the tape. It was thus too late for us to carry it in our last week's issue, for the paper was already off the machines, ready for distribution on Friday. The dailies carried the story the next morning, and immediately our 'phone bell started to ring and continued ringing most of the day, from admirers of Al all over the country, only too ready to believe that it wasn't true. It was astonishing proof of the tremendous esteem in which he was held, not only in the profession but amongst the general public.

GREAT-HEARTEDNESS

It was an index, too, of the man's own great-heartedness. I have never met Al Bowlly without feeling his own innate sincerity, without realising that his destiny in the world was to charm people with his voice, and to lift them for a few moments out of the drabness of their workaday lives. Al really lived for his job. He lived and dreamed of it, and nobody was more conscious of the debt he owed to his Maker for giving him the gift of song. There have been times when I have smiled at the rather melodramatic way in which he would throw up his arms in the street and say "Thank God, it's terrific!" when I asked how his act was going.

Now I know that behind the facade which we knew as Al Bowlly was a deeply religious man. I know that he carried a message of destiny, and that if there are any among you who might feel that such a description of a singer of popular songs hardly warrants such a conclusion, let me tell you just one more astonishing fact in the awful story. The very last record broadcast by the BBC of Al singing, was the one in which he sang with Ken Johnson's band . . .'

On Saturday 26 April, nine days after he died, Al went to his last resting place, a communal grave at the Westminster City Council Cemetery, Uxbridge Road, Hanwell in West London. Among those present at the funeral was Chick Henderson, the singer who had beaten Al in the popularity stakes during the months before he died, and his wife Marjie. Archmin James Virvos, Dean of the Greek Orthodox Cathedral in London and the second most senior member of this Church in England, conducted the funeral service which had been arranged by Helen Bevan. It is interesting to

119

note that the Book of Burials of the Greek Orthodox Church shows 'Alexander Pavlos' as Al's name, indicating that he clung to his Greek origins throughout his life.

A later memorial service in May of that year was held at the Greek Orthodox Church in Bayswater. A press report at the time stated that Marjie wanted it recorded that Jimmy Mesene had arranged it.

Al left his possessions to his mother. However, apart from money, there were really very few personal possessions as Al always travelled light. He is reputed to have given his guitar to Jimmy Mesene and Lew Stone received a few Monseigneur records. Unlike many artistes, Al kept no letters, contracts, press cuttings or anything of that sort. Helen says that she 'lost everything' in the Dukes Court flat, and after Al died she moved back with her mother.

His death certificate erroneously names him as Albert *Alex* Bowlly but correctly describes him as a 'professional singer'. Another mistake appears in the records at the Westminster City Council Cemetery at Hanwell, where the entry relating to Al reads BOWLLY, A. E. Next to Al's name was the symbol ✖, which was to distinguish those who were air raid victims.

As the name BOWLLY had an unusual spelling – I have never heard of it being spelt that way by anyone not a member of Al's family – it was often misspelt in the press and in articles about him during his lifetime. The most common mistake was to spell it *Bowley*.

The Letters of Administration of Al's estate were given to his solicitor, Mr Kenneth H. Thompson of Piccadilly, at the Principal Probate Registry at Llandudno in October 1942.

The gross value of the estate was £1163.2s.8d, £867s.0s.8d after death duties. At the date of death, Al had only £3.10s.9d in his bank account. The bulk of the estate came from the realisation of the insurance policy he had taken out with the National Mutual Life Association of Australia, which was worth around £1000. The annual premium, incidentally, was £49.2s.6d.

Kenneth Thompson inserted the statutory advertisements in the *Times* of 16 September 1942 and in the *London Gazette* of 11 September 1942 with no response.

However a Tax Assessment was received for £500 from the Inland Revenue which was issued as Al had failed to reply to departmental letters about his royalties from HMV. Mr Thompson later had the assessment reduced to £45.6s.3d after he had proved that the royalties were not as substantial as the Revenue had originally estimated.

To partly compensate for this, a cheque for £10.9s.4d was received from the Mechanical Copyright Protection Society of which Al was a member.

Eventually £720 was sent to Al's mother who was known as Mary Bowlly by the solicitor. Mary Bowlly, incidentally, died on 2 June 1949 from cancer of the colon. Mish Bowlly subsequently became Al's heir and in the late

1970s and early 1980s had been sent around £1000 in royalties from Al's records.

During the last few years of his life, Al had been under financial pressure. Following the loss from the Rhythm Makers band, he had been presented with a claim for maintenance from Marjie and had later been in dispute with Odham's Press. Nevertheless, he let his family back in South Africa believe he was 'comfortably-off'.

After Al's death his partner, Jimmy Mesene carried on working alone, adopting as his signature tune *Brother Can You Spare a Dime?* as a tribute to Al. However, the act didn't last very long and Jimmy seems to have faded into obscurity. His death was reported in the mid-1950s.

In July 1942 *Melody Maker* carried a letter to the Editor from an Al Bowlly fan complaining that no tombstone had been erected to Al. All there was in the cemetery was a barren piece of land. The writer of the letter called on other fans of Al for a subscription to cover the cost of a memorial.

Two weeks later it was reported that subscriptions had poured into their office. However, the *Melody Maker* had discovered that a subscription was unnecessary as Jimmy Mesene had made arrangements for a tombstone to be erected. These plans did not materialise for Al was buried in a communal grave and as Jimmy was not related to Al he could not get the necessary permission to carry out his excellent intention.

In the end a tombstone for all those buried in the communal grave was erected and to this day no special memorial to Al exists.

CHAPTER FOURTEEN

Moonlight on the Highway

After Al's death, the battle of London continued and he was soon a forgotten man. In the face of the common enemy the war progressed and in its later years claimed another victim – Chick Henderson, the singer who had previously attended Bowlly's funeral.

In America, Frank Sinatra had attained stardom and the era of the popular singer was upon us. The word crooner was a relic of the past. The dance bands never re-established themselves. Within ten years rock 'n' roll and pop music as we know it today had begun.

A question frequently asked is 'Had Bowlly survived the war, what would he have become?' And the answer that frequently occurs is 'He would have become a star in the fullest sense of the word and even have outshone Crosby', although it is difficult to envisage.

Al Bowlly was part of the dance band era. He had not established himself as an actor, film star or even just a singing star in his own right. Whereas America had Bing Crosby, Britain had no similar position for any entertainer to occupy. Bowlly, the superlative band singer was Britain's nearest thing to Crosby the singing star.

After the war, this period had ended. I think if the post-war career of band singer Sam Browne is considered, some idea of what might have happened to Al Bowlly will emerge. Sam Browne carried on into the early 1950s – but he was not then a star. He soon drifted into obscurity, working in a betting office before fully retiring. If Al had survived the war and been able to have maintained his voice as it was in the early 1940s (remembering that his voice was weakening anyway), he might have kept going in the same way as Donald Peers did. But it is highly unlikely that he would ever have topped the bill on Sunday Night at the London Palladium.

Returning to the popular music scene of the 1950s, coinciding with the event of rock 'n' roll came the era of microgroove records. Soon no one wanted 78s anymore. They could be picked up in junk shops and market places for a penny or twopence each. Many who now possess leading collections of 78s obtained theirs in this way and many post-war collectors were collecting Al Bowlly records much more seriously than people had done in the singer's heyday. But as far as the general public was concerned, few people remembered Al Bowlly. Indeed when the Noble/Bowlly recording of *Lady of Spain* was reissued in the US in 1947, the voices of two other singers were dubbed over Al so that on the version put on sale, poor old Al could not be distinguished! However, the BBC would occasionally broadcast a record of, or even a tribute to Al.

During the 1950s one or two singers have tried to recapture the Bowlly voice. For example at the Cricklewood Palais de Danse in London, the band leader, Jan Wildman, often sang *Brother Can You Spare a Dime?* in reminiscent style, although the best known Bowlly 'sound-alike' was Steve Conway. Many people consider that the late Steve Conway copied, or at least, sounded like Al. On certain vowel sounds there is a similarity, but he can sound just as 'Jolsonish' as 'Bowllyish'. But many people did consider Steve to be Al's replacement. Even Lew Stone considered employing Steve if he had re-formed his successful dance band after the war.

However, in the main, until the nostalgia boom of the 1960s came about, Al was still a forgotten man. The 1960s brought with them LP re-issues of original 78s, specialist nostalgia magazines and radio programmes. Millions of listeners still tune in weekly to BBC radio to listen to the 'Dance Band Days' in which Al Bowlly is frequently heard.

As regards television, some readers may remember the ITV play about a young man obsessed with the voice of Al Bowlly. The play was televised in April 1969, called *Moonlight on the Highway* and was written by Dennis Potter. It did, in fact, win converts to Al Bowlly's music as many of his records were featured, as well as an extract of the film in which he sang *My Melancholy Baby*. In addition, Al was frequently seen in the ITV programmes 'All our Yesterdays' and 'Looks Familiar'.

Many of those who were still alive and who were associated with Al came together in 1976 for an hour long BBC TV tribute to Al, entitled 'Impressions of Al Bowlly'. Taking part in this were Roy Fox, Joyce Stone (Lew's widow), Ray Noble and musicians Joe Crossman, Nat Gonella, Sid Colin, Tiny Winters and Monia Liter. The tribute was much criticised at the time, especially as it showed no film of, or played no record of Al himself. The main part of the tribute was an impersonation of Al by modern day actor Stuart Damon. The programme did little in bringing forth new facts about Al or dispelling any of the myths. However, it was certainly the most elaborate tribute ever made to him.

In the late 1970s there was a series of plays by Dennis Potter entitled *Pennies from Heaven*. This was set in the 1930s and every episode included lots of original records from that era. And the voice of Al Bowlly was heard far more than any other singer, therefore winning a lot of converts to Al among younger people who were captivated by his voice.

Radio fans may remember the 1960s as the age of the pirate radio stations broadcasting continuous music from high seas. One of the many tributes to Al Bowlly broadcast on radio stations all over the world was transmitted by

Radio 390 in the Thames Estuary. It was entitled 'They Called Me Al' and was one of the most dramatic Bowlly tributes ever to be broadcast.

In more recent years, the BBC have also broadcast tributes at the anniversary of Bowlly's death. There were tributes to Al in the series 'Dance Band Days', broadcast in April 1976 and 1977 and compered by Alan Dell. In 1981 to mark the fortieth anniversary of Al's death many further tributes were broadcast. Also in the 1980s an Al Bowlly film clip was shown in both series of the BBC TV production 'Turns' which featured variety acts of the 1930s.

Not only have the broadcasters played their part in preserving the name of Al Bowlly but the record companies have done their bit as well. Both EMI and Decca brought out many LP re-issues of Al's original 78s including a complete set of all the Noble/Bowlly HMV sessions. In many cases the sound quality of the LP re-issues have been immensely improved in the course of re-mastering the records. The annoying surface noise on the old 78s has almost completely been eliminated on the more recent re-issues.

Nevertheless, despite the LP re-issues of Al Bowlly material his original 78 rpm discs are still in demand from an international army of record collectors. Bids for Bowlly originals are consistently among the highest received by record auctioneers for any artists. With Bing Crosby and Al Jolson, Bowlly is one of the three most collected artistes on pre-war 78s.

Perhaps, as this story nears its end, readers may be wondering what happened to some of the people who were associated with Al Bowlly during his lifetime. The demise has already been recorded of Al's partner of the day JIMMY MESENE, so to conclude there follows a brief account of some of Al's other associates:

EDGAR ADELER, the first man to employ Al as a professional musician died in 1985. He continued to work as a pianist and cabaret artiste well into his eighties. He had also written his autobiography.

Similarly writing his autobiography is Negro trumpeter ARTHUR BRIGGS, the leader of one of the first bands Al ever recorded with back in Berlin in 1927.

FRED ELIZALDE shortly after his band at the Savoy Hotel broke up, went abroad and in recent years has been involved with the broadcasting and composing of serious music.

LEN FILLIS with whom Al recorded profusely in the early 1930s subsequently worked with much success in Australia and South Africa. He died after an illness in Johannesburg in the early 1950s.

The man who got Al started again in England in 1930, ROY FOX, gave up bandleading in the 1950s and went into personal management. He died after a long retirement in 1982.

The pianist in the Roy Fox Band destined to become one of England's most prominent bandleaders was LEW STONE. After the war, he never re-formed an orchestra comparable to his pre-war outfits. He made a few 'Music While You Work' broadcasts, and died after a heart attack in February 1969.

As regards RAY NOBLE, he retired gracefully after realising that the post-war music scene was not for him. He spent his old age in his home in California but died in a London hospital during a visit to this country in April 1978.

In his post America years, Al worked a lot for GERALDO who carried on working after the war on radio and television, making records up to his death in 1974.

Another band leader Al worked for in the later 1930s was REGINALD WILLIAMS who, after the war, remained in the entertainment world as a manager. Still very much alive and well, Reg is now semi-retired, writing a book and with plans to revive his 'Futurists'.

And finally, Al's brother MISH BOWLLY, is in Johannesburg, teaching music and has been an invaluable help throughout the preparation of this book.

As to Al himself, his remains are at the City of Westminster Cemetery in London which is, at the time of writing, the only memorial to him. During the 1960s, the bronze name plates and other metal fittings were stripped from the tomb by grave-robbers, but, within a short space of time the desecration of Al's grave was put right. The names are now chiselled in stone. No special mention is made of Al's name – it appears along the top row as simply BOWLLY A. A. The graveside consists of a grassy plot about 40 feet by 10 feet and is bounded by a kerbstone surround. The whitestone memorial is impressive because of its simplicity. It has a tall column surmounted by a cross.

And so we come to the end of our story of one of the most interesting and fascinating personalities in popular music's history – Al Bowlly.

Let it finish with a few words from Ray Noble, spoken in a post-war interview:

> 'Even after all these dangerous years I still get many enquiries about Al Bowlly. And sometimes when a middle-aged father says to me "I first met my wife the night we danced to your band and Al sung *Goodnight Sweetheart* – and we've never forgotten it", then I feel that both Al and I have contributed in our small way to other people's happiness. And how I wish he was here now to share that feeling.'

Discography

The Discography which follows lists every known recording which contains the voice of Al Bowlly. The recordings are listed in alphabetical order of the song title. The vast majority of entries relate to normal commercial gramophone records. However, we have also included non-commercial items such as film sound tracks, radio transcription discs, air-checks (recordings taken from radio broadcasts) and private recordings. The Discography is the most comprehensive listing of Al Bowlly recordings ever produced.

There are five columns in the Discography.

Column 1
This contains the full title of the recording. Al Bowlly's presence on a few titles has yet to be confirmed. Such items are shown as '(unconfirmed)'. Where Bowlly sings in a language other than English, this is also shown in brackets, e.g. (in Afrikaans).

Column 2
This contains the name of the artiste under which the recording was originally made. In most cases this is the name of a dance band. In other cases the recordings were issued under Bowlly's own name. When this is the case 'AB' is shown as the artiste. Details of accompanists or musical directors names are given, where known, although these details did not always appear on the original record label. The abbreviations used in this column are:

AB	Al Bowlly	Haw Sing	Hawaiian Singers
acc	Accompanied by	NMDO	New Mayfair Dance
acc orc dir	Accompanying		Orchestra
	orchestra directed by	Mons	Monseigneur
ahb	And His Band	Orc	Orchestra
aho	And His Orchestra	p	Piano
duet LA	Duet with Les Allen	Sav Syn	Savoy Syncopaters
Haw Pla	Hawaiian Players	vn	Violin

It is not considered appropriate here to list all the personnel of the accompanying bands and groups. However, it is thought that the following details about the leaders of bands included in the discography, where it is not obvious, would be of interest.

LEN FILLIS used many pseudonyms for his groups. Those included in this discography are: Brooklyn Broadcasters, Ferrachini's Hawaiian Band, Hawaiian Octet, Hawaiian Quartet, Hawaiian Serenaders, Honolulu Quartet, Honolulu Serenaders, Earl Melville and his Hawaiians, Linn Milford and his Hawaiian Players/Singers, Palm Beach Hawaiians, Phantom Players, Al Vocale and his Crooners, Waikiki Serenaders.

ROY FOX was leader of the Rhythm Maniacs as included in this discography.

CARROLL GIBBONS was leader of the Savoy Hotel Orpheans who also recorded as The Masqueraders.

HARRY HUDSON was house bandleader for the Edison Bell Radio label. Some of the records were issued under his own name. Others were issued as: Blue Jays, Deauville Dance Band, Radio Melody Boys, Radio Rhythm Boys, Radio Rhythm Five, Tuff Guys.

RAY NOBLE was leader of the house band for the HMV label from 1929–34. Many of the records were issued under his own name. Others were issued as: Night Club Kings, London Mayfair Orchestra, New Mayfair Dance Orchestra, New Mayfair Novelty Orchestra, New Mayfair Orchestra (unless indicated differently in Discography), Novelty Orchestra.

LEW STONE was director of the Durium Dance Band.

Column 3

This contains details of the place where each recording was made. The abbreviations used in this column are:

Ber	Berlin, Germany
Hay	Hayes, Middlesex, England
Lon	London, England
NY	New York, USA

Column 4

This contains the date on which each recording was made. Where the day or the month of the recording is unknown, a hyphen (––) is shown. The century of the date is not shown.

Column 5

This contains details of the original issue in the form of record label followed by catalogue number. In the majority of cases this is a 78 rpm record.

Where an item was not commercially issued at the time and has since been issued on microgroove a plus sign (+) follows the catalogue number. An asterisk (*) against the catalogue number of an item not issued under Al Bowlly as principal artiste indicates that his name nevertheless appears on the record label. The absence of details for label and catalogue number indicates that the recording has not been commercially issued.

The abbreviations used in this column are:

Record Labels.
All UK labels and referring to 78 rpm records unless otherwise stated.

Air	Aircheck (American, microgroove)		export label for Deutsche Grammophon
BB	Blue Bird (American label)	Hal	Halcyon (microgroove)
Bdcst	Broadcast	HMV	His Masters Voice
Brun	Brunswick	Hom	Homocord (German label)
Cel	Celebrity		
Col	Columbia	Imp	Imperial
Dec	Decca (No. prefix, American label, others UK 78 rpm and microgroove)	JA	Jazz Archives (American Microgroove)
		Lon	London (microgroove)
		May	Mayfair
Dom	Dominion	Met	Metropole
EBR	Edison Bell Radio	Oct	Octocross
EBW	Edison Bell Winner	Pan	Panachord
EMI	Electrical and Musical Industries (microgroove)	Parl	Parlophone
		Pic	Piccadilly
		Pres	President (microgroove)
Fan	Fanfare (American, microgroove)	Reg	Regal
Film	Filmophone	Sav	Saville (microgroove)
DG/Pol	Deutsche Grammophon (German label) and Polydor, the	Vic	Victor (American label)
		WR	World Records (microgroove)

Types of recording.
All recordings were for commercial issue unless one of the following abbreviations is shown at the end of this column.

AC	Air check (a recording from a radio broadcast)	RT	Radio Transcription (a recording originally made for broadcasting only)
FS	Film sound track		
PR	Private recording		

Title	Artiste	Place	Date	Original Issue
Actions Speak Louder Than Words	Masqueraders	Lon	14 Jan 32	Col CB-409
Adeline	Jay Wilbur ahb	Lon	-- Oct 30	Imp 2355
Adios	Roy Fox ahb	Lon	4 Feb 32	Dec F-2805
Adorable	Lew Stone and the Mons Band	Lon	15 Sep 33	Dec F-3676
After All, You're All I'm After	Ray Noble aho	Lon	27 Apr 34	HMV B-6485
After My Laughter Came Tears (unconfirmed)	Billy Bartholomew's Delphians	Ber	-- May 28	DG/Pol 21599
After My Laughter Came Tears	Fred Elizalde and his Music	Lon	25 Jul 28	Brun rejected
After The Sun Kissed The World Goodbye	Fred Elizalde's Rhythmicians	Lon	4 Dec 29	Met 1241, Oct 367
Ain't She Sweet?	Fred Bird, The Salon Symphonic Jazz Band	Ber	12 Sep 27	Hom 4-2389
Ain't She Sweet?	Arthur Briggs' Sav Syn Orc	Ber	-- Oct 27	DG/Pol 21124*
Ain't That A Grand And Glorious Feeling	Arthur Briggs' Sav Syn Orc	Ber	-- Oct 27	DG/Pol 21135
Allah's Holiday	Night Club Kings	Lon	17 Jul 30	HMV rejected
All Ashore	Lew Stone ahb	Lon	28 Nov 38	Dec F-6890*
All Day Long	AB	Ber	22 Sep 27	Hom 4-2414
Alleenig (in Afrikaans)	AB acc Albert Diggenhof (p)	Hay	30 Jan 30	HMV FJ-100
All I Do Is Dream Of You	Ray Noble aho	Lon	11 Jul 34	HMV B-6508
All I Want Is You	John Abriani's Six	Ber	20 Jan 28	Hom 4-2532
All of a Sudden	Roy Fox ahb	Lon	23 Sep 32	Dec F-3181
All of Me	Durium Dance Band	Lon	15 Mar 32	Durium EN-8
All Over Italy	Ray Noble aho (with chorus)	Lon	24 May 33	HMV B-6364
All Through The Night	Roy Fox ahb	Lon	5 Mar 31	Dec F-2249
All Through The Night	Marius B. Winter and his Dance Orc	Lon	-- Mar 31	Bdcst 3034
Alma Mia	Roy Fox ahb (with chorus)	Lon	1 Apr 31	Dec F-2292
Aloha Oe	Hawaiian Quartet	Lon	9 Sep 30	Dec rejected
Aloha Oe	Hawaiian Quartet	Lon	24 Sep 30	Dec F-2066
And So Goodbye	Ray Noble aho	Lon	9 Nov 33	HMV B-6422
And So I Married The Girl	Lew Stone and the Mons Band	Lon	5 Apr 33	Dec F-3535
Antoinette	Lew Stone ahb	Lon	-- -- 32	FS

Title	Artiste	Place	Date	Original Issue
Any Broken Hearts To Mend?	Lew Stone ahb	Lon	28 Nov 38	Dec F-6891*
Any Broken Hearts To Mend?	Geraldo aho	Lon	16 Dec 38	HMV BD-5443*
Are You Happy?	Arthur Briggs' Sav Syn Orc	Ber	– – Oct 27	DG/Pol 21130
Are You Prepared (To Be True)?	Roy Fox ahb	Lon	9 Sep 32	Dec F-3152
Are You Thinking Of Me Tonight?	John Abriani's Six	Ber	18 Jan 28	Hom 4-2612
Arm In Arm	Maurice Winnick aho	Lon	26 Mar 40	HMV BD-5583*
As Long As I Live	Lew Stone ahb	Lon	3 Aug 34	Dec F-5132
At Last I'm Happy	Waldorfians dir Howard Godfrey	Lon	– – Jun 31	Empire E-8
Auf Wiedersehen, My Dear	Durium Dance Band	Lon	20 Apr 32	Durium EN-12
Auf Wiedersehen, My Dear	AB ('Al Bowlly Remembers')	Lon	11 Nov 38	Dec F-6916
Au Revoir, But Not Goodbye	AB acc orc dir Ronnie Munro	Lon	5 Oct 39	HMV BD-762
Awend (in Afrikaans)	AB as Jannie Viljoen acc Claude Ivy (p)	Lon	30 Oct 30	Dec rejected
Balloons	Lew Stone and the Mons Band	Lon	29 Nov 32	Dec F-3314
Banditlied (in Afrikaans)	AB	Hay	14 Jul 30	HMV FJ-133
Barcarolle (Tales of Hoffman)	New Mayfair Orc (duet with Suzanne Botterill) 'Venetian Nights'	Lon	6 Apr 33	HMV C-2565
Basin Street Blues	AB acc orc dir Ray Noble	NY	15 Mar 35	HMV BD-226, Vic 25007
Bathing In The Sunshine	Roy Fox ahb	Lon	5 Mar 31	Dec F-2250
Beat O' My Heart	Ray Noble aho	Lon	31 May 34	HMV B-6491
Beat O' My Heart	Lew Stone ahb	Lon	15 Jun 34	Dec F-5018*
Beautiful Lady In Blue, A	Ray Noble aho	NY	9 Dec 35	Vic 25209*
Because I Love You	AB acc Fred Bird (vn); Edgar Adeler (p)	Ber	23 Sep 27	Hom 4-2418
Because It's Love	Lew Stone ahb	Lon	23 Mar 34	Dec F-3942*
Bedtime Story, A	Ray Noble and the NMDO	Lon	11 Oct 32	HMV B-6250, Vic 24226

Title	Artiste	Place	Date	Original Issue
Bei Mir Bist Du Schoen	Maurice Winnick and his Sweet Music	Lon	29 Dec 37	Dec F-6591
Bei Mir Bist Du Schoen	AB acc orc dir Ronnie Munro	Lon	4 Jan 38	HMV BD-493
Bei Mir Bist Du Schoen	Lew Stone ahb	Lon	2 Feb 38	AC
Bella Bambina	AB acc orc dir Ronnie Munro	Lon	21 Dec 39	HMV BD-808
Bell Bottom Trousers	Jack Leon ahb (as Jerome Joy ahb on Simcha)	Lon	––Jun 31	Pic 782, Oct 614, Simcha 10001
Belle Of Barcelona	Radio Melody Boys	Lon	––Aug 31	EBR 1535
Belle Of Barcelona	NMDO	Lon	14 Aug 31	HMV B-6055
Beloved (unconfirmed)	Billy Bartholomew's Delphians	Ber	––Jun 28	DG/Pol 21663
Bench In The Park, A	Harry Hudsons's Melody Men (duet LA)	Lon	––Sep 30	EBW 5160
Be Still My Heart	AB acc orc dir Victor Young	NY	30 Oct 34	Dec F-5326, 293
Betty Co-ed	Roy Fox ahb	Lon	15 Apr 31	Dec F-2312
Between A Kiss And A Sigh	Geraldo aho	Lon	7 Mar 39	HMV BD-5468*
Between The Devil And The Deep Blue Sea	Roy Fox ahb (with chorus)	Lon	9 Feb 31	Dec F-2240
Beware Of Love	Marius B. Winter and his Dance Orc	Lon	––Nov 30	Bdcst 2600
Big Chief De Sota	Ray Noble aho	NY	25 May 36	HMV BD-5095*, Vic 25346*
Blackpool Walk, The	Felix Mendelssohn aho	Lon	1 Jul 38	Dec F-6726*
Blazin' The Trail	Ray Noble aho	NY	19 Mar 36	HMV BD-5072*, Vic 25282*
Blow, Blow Thou Winter Wind	Ken 'Snakehips' Johnson and his West Indian Orc (with the Henderson Twins)	Lon	24 Apr 40	HMV BD-5592*
Blue Hawaii	AB	Lon	5 Jul 37	HMV BD-440
Blue Is The Night	Paramount Rhythm Boys (duet LA)	Lon	––Sep 30	EBW 5161
Blue Moon	AB acc by orc dir Ray Noble	NY	12 Jan 35	Vic 24849
Blue Pacific Moonlight	Linn Milford and his Haw Pla (duet LA)	Lon	19 Sep 30	Reg MR-187

Title	Artiste	Place	Date	Original Issue
Blue Prelude	Lew Stone and the Mons Band	Lon	15 Sep 33	Dec F-3675
Blues In My Heart	Ray Noble and the NMDO	Lon	12 Feb 32	HMV B-6147, Vic 25141
Blue Skies	AB acc Edgar Adeler (p)	Ber	18 Aug 27	Hom 4-2386
Bonjour, Mam'selle	Ray Noble aho	NY	10 May 35	HMV BD-192*, Vic 25040*
Brighter Than The Sun	Ray Noble aho	Lon	8 Dec 32	HMV B-6302, Vic 24314
Brighter Than The Sun	Lew Stone and the Mons Band	Lon	23 Dec 32	Dec F-3373*
Brivele de Mame – see 'Letter to my Mother'				
Brother, Can You Spare A Dime?	Ray Noble aho	Lon	17 Mar 33	HMV test
Brother, Can You Spare A Dime?	Lew Stone ahb 'Lew Stone Favourites'	Lon	1 Dec 33	Dec K-715
Brother, Can You Spare A Dime?	Lew Stone ahb 'Lew Stone Favourites'	Lon	12 Dec 33	AC
Brother, Can You Spare A Dime?	Unknown acc	Lon	–– Jan 38	AC
Brother, Can You Spare A Dime?	AB acc George Scott-Wood (pipe organ)	Lon	25 May 38	HMV rejected
Bubbling Over With Love	Roy Fox ahb	Lon	21 Apr 31	Dec F-2328
Bubbling Over With Love	Len Fillis and his Novelty Orc	Lon	6 May 31	Col DB-549
Bubbling Over With Love	Jack Leon ahb	Lon	–– Jun 31	Pic 802
But Definitely	Ray Noble aho	NY	25 May 36	HMV BD-5091*, Vic 25336*
Butterflies In The Rain	Ray Noble aho	Lon	31 Jan 33	HMV B-6316, Vic 24296
By An Old Pagoda	Lew Stone ahb	Lon	21 Apr 38	Dec F-6663*
By Die Vaal Rivier (in Taal dialect)	AB as Jannie Viljoen acc Claude Ivy (p)	Lon	13 Oct 30	Dec rejected
Bye-Bye Blues	Waikiki Serenaders (duet LA)	Lon	–– Nov 30	Bdcst 644
By My Side	Roy Fox ahb	Lon	5 May 31	Dec F-2341
By the Fireside	Ray Noble and the NMDO	Lon	8 Jan 32	HMV B-6131, Vic 25141

Title	Artiste	Place	Date	Original Issue
By The Fireside	Durium Dance Band	Lon	15 Mar 32	Durium EN-0
By The Fireside	New Mayfair Orc	Lon	27 May 32	HMV B-4208
By The Fireside	Ray Noble aho 'Ray Noble Medley'	NY	13 May 35	Lon HMG-5019+RT
By The Old Oak Tree	Al Bowlly and Ella Logan acc Claude Ivy (p)	Lon	24 Nov 30	Dec F-2206
By The River Sainte Marie	Roy Fox ahb	Lon	16 Jun 31	Dec rejected
By The River Sainte Marie	Deauville Dance Band	Lon	–– Sep 31	EBR 1558
By The Vaal River – see 'By Die Vaal Rivier'				
Call It A Day	Roy Fox ahb	Lon	9 Sep 32	Dec F-3151
Can't We Be Friends?	Roy Fox ahb	Lon	16 Jan 31	Dec F-2220
Can't We Meet Again?	NMDO	Lon	20 Feb 33	HMV B-6320
Can't We Meet Again?	Scott-Wood Accordion Quartet	Lon	3 Apr 33	Parl R-1469
Can't We Talk It Over?	Roy Fox ahb	Lon	13 Apr 32	Dec F-2923
Can't We Talk It Over?	Durium Dance Band	Lon	20 Apr 32	Durium EN-13
Can't You Hear Me Say 'I Love You'?	John Abriani's Six	Ber	20 Jan 28	Hom 4-2532
Can't I – see 'I Can Dream Can't I?'				
Careless	AB acc orc dir Billy Munn	Lon	15 Feb 40	HMV BD-828
Carelessly	AB	Lon	19 Jun 37	HMV BD-434
C'est Vous (unconfirmed)	Billy Batholomew's Delphians	Ber	–– May 28	DG/Pol 21596
Champagne Waltz	AB acc Claude Bampton (p)	Lon	–––– 39	PR
Changes	Billy Batholomew's Delphians	Ber	–– May 28	DG/Pol 21599
Change Partners	Geraldo aho	Lon	–––– 39	Sav SVL-168+RT
Chatterbox	Maurice Winnick aho	Lon	1 Mar 40	HMV BD-5572
Cheer Up And Smile	Paramount Rhythm Boys (duet LA)	Lon	–– Sep 30	EBW 5161
Cherie, C'est Vous	Roy Fox ahb	Lon	18 Aug 31	Dec F-2451*
Close Your Eyes	Lew Stone ahb	Lon	1 Dec 33	Dec F-3783
Close Your Eyes	Ray Noble aho	Lon	7 Dec 33	HMV B-6441
Clouds	Ray Noble aho	NY	9 Feb 35	HMV BD-147* Vic 24865*

Title	Artiste	Place	Date	Original Issue
Coal Black Mammy	New Mayfair Orchestra	Lon	14 Jul 31	HMV B-3944
Coffee In The Morning	Lew Stone ahb	Lon	15 Feb 34	Dec F-3905
Colorado Sunset	Geraldo aho	Lon	3 Dec 38	HMV BD-5438*
Colorado Sunset	Geraldo aho	Lon	—— 39	Hal HAL-4+RT
Come On, Be Happy	Jack Jackson aho	Lon	24 Feb 33	HMV B-6330
Concentratin'	Roy Fox ahb	Lon	22 Feb 32	Dec F-2839
Considerin'	Arthur Lally aho (as Jack Holmes aho on Mayfair)	Lon	29 Sep 32	Dec F-3187, May G-2202
Could Be	Geraldo aho	Lon	7 Mar 39	HMV BD-5468*
Couple Of Fools In Love, A	Ray Noble aho	Lon	20 Jun 33	HMV B-6366
Cuban Love Song	Ferrachini's Hawaiian Band (duet LA)	Lon	—— Nov 30	Bdcst 2605
Cuddle Up Close	Eddie Pola and Company 'America Calling'	Lon	25 Jul 33	Col DX-499
Daar Is Geen Ron In Die Hemel (in Afrikaans)	AB	Hay	10 Oct 30	HMV FJ-120
Dance Hall Doll	Roy Fox ahb	Lon	3 Sep 31	Dec F-2486
Dance Of The Cuckoos	Rudy Starita with Arthur Lally aho	Lon	21 Sep 32	Dec F-3186
Dancing In The Dark	AB ('Al Bowlly Remembers')	Lon	11 Nov 38	Dec F-6916
Dancing With Tears In My Eyes	Aldwych Players dir Jay Wilbur	Lon	2 Aug 30	Victory 255
Dark Clouds	Lew Stone ahb	Lon	29 Dec 33	Dec F-3826
Dark Eyes	AB acc ord dir Ronnie Munro	Lon	11 May 39	HMV BD-709
Day You Came Along, The	Lew Stone ahb	Lon	24 Oct 33	Dec F-3722
Dear Little Gadabout	AB acc Heinz Lewy (p)	Ber	18 Nov 27	Hom 4-2459
Dear, When I Met You	Blue Jays	Lon	—— Nov 31	EBR 1585
Deep In A Dream	Geraldo aho	Lon	3 Feb 39	HMV BD-5457*
Did You Ever See A Dream Walking?	Ray Noble aho	Lon	20 Dec 33	HMV B-6441
Dinah	Jock McDermott ahb	Lon	5 Jan 32	EBW 5468
Dinah	Ray Noble aho	Lon	25 Apr 33	HMV test
Dinner At Eight	Ray Noble aho	Lon	12 Oct 33	HMV B-6409

134

Title	Artiste	Place	Date	Original Issue
Dinner For One, Please, James	Ray Noble aho	NY	14 Nov 35	Vic 25187*
Don't Change	Lew Stone ahb	Lon	24 Oct 33	Dec F-3821
Don't Say Goodbye	Ray Noble and the NMDO	Lon	11 Oct 32	HMV B-6251
Don't Say Goodnight	Bohemians, dir Walter Goehr	Lon	18 Apr 34	Col DX-583
Do The Black Bottom With Me	Arthur Briggs' Sav Syn Orc	Ber	–– Oct 27	DG/Pol 21122
Down And Out Blues	Lew Stone ahb (with Sid Colin)	Lon	12 Aug 38	Dec F-6743*
Down And Out Blues	Lew Stone ahb (with Sid Colin)	Lon	27 Aug 38	AC
Down By The River	Ray Noble aho	NY	9 Feb 35	HMV BD-140*, Vic 24879*
Down Sunnyside Lane	NMDO	Lon	31 Oct 31	HMV B-6091
Dreaming	AB acc orc dir Ronnie Munro	Lon	7 Mar 40	HMV BD-834
Dreaming A Dream	Ray Noble aho	Lon	30 Aug 34	HMV B-6520, Vic 24850
Dream Of You, A	AB	Ber	22 Sep 27	Hom 4-2411
Dreams That Don't Grow Old	Ray Noble and the NMDO	Lon	8 Jun 32	HMV B-6192
Dreamy Serenade	Ray Noble aho	Lon	11 Jul 34	HMV B-6510
Dreamy Serenade (a different song to the one above)	AB acc Claude Bampton (p)	Lon	–– –– 39	PR
Driftin' Tide	Ray Noble aho	Lon	18 Jul 34	HMV B-6511, Vic 25006
Drums In My Heart	Arthur Lally aho	Lon	30 Jun 32	Dec F-3057
Eadie Was A Lady	Lew Stone ahb	Lon	29 Dec 33	Dec F-3825
Easy Come, Easy Go	Lew Stone ahb	Lon	15 Jun 34	Dec F-5018*
Easy To Love	Ray Noble aho	NY	25 Sep 36	HMV BD-5147*, Vic 25422*
Easy To Love	Ray Noble aho	NY	7 Dec 36	Lon HMG 5027+ RT
Echo Of A Song	Roy Fox ahb	Lon	19 May 32	Dec rejected
Echo Of A Song	Ray Noble and the NMDO	Lon	8 Jun 32	HMV B-6193
Echo Of A Song	Roy Fox ahb	Lon	10 Jun 32	Dec F-3015, Brun 6457
Ek Dink Altyd Aan Jou (in Afrikaans)	AB as Jannie Viljoen acc Claude Ivy (p)	Lon	30 Oct 30	Dec rejected

Title	Artiste	Place	Date	Original Issue
Eleven More Months And Ten More Days	Tuff Guys	Lon	8 Dec 31	EBR 1586
Eleven More Months And Ten More Days	AB and the Radio Rhythm Five	Lon	9 Dec 31	EBW 5440
Empty Saddles	Ray Noble aho	NY	25 May 36	HMV BD-5095*, Vic 25346*
Ending With A Kiss	Lew Stone ahb	Lon	25 Apr 34	Dec F-3979*
Evening – see 'Awend'				
Every Day's a Holiday	Al Bowlly aho	NY	3 Dec 37	BB B-7319*
Every Day's A Lucky Day	Arthur Lally aho	Lon	30 Jun 32	Dec F-3057
Ev'ry Little Kindness (Makes An Angel Smile)	Linn Milford and his Haw Sing	Lon	2 Jul 30	Reg MR-197
Ev'ry Little Thing I Do	AB acc Heinz Lewy (p)	Ber	18 Nov 27	Hom 4-2460
Everyone Should Have A Sweetheart	Lew Stone ahb	Lon	3 Oct 38	Dec F-6811
Everything I Have Is Yours	AB	Lon	4 Jan 34	Dec F-3853
Everything's Been Done Before	AB acc orc dir Ray Noble	NY	15 Mar 35	HMV BD-226, Vic 25004
Experiment	Ray Noble aho	Lon	12 Oct 33	HMV B-6408, Vic 25006
Experiment	Lew Stone ahb	Lon	3 Nov 33	Dec F-3734
Faded Summer Love, A	AB acc Harry Hudson (p)	Lon	13 Jan 32	EBW 5470
Faint Harmony	Lew Stone ahb	Lon	15 Feb 34	Dec F-3883
Fair And Warmer	Ray Noble aho	Lon	28 Jun 34	HMV B-6503
Falling In Love	New Cumberland Dance Orc	Lon	–– Jan 32	Film 378
Falling In Love Again	Al Vocale and his Crooners (duet LA)	Lon	–– Sep 30	EBR 1389
Falling In Love Again	New Mayfair Orc	Lon	24 Mar 31	HMV B-3836
Fancy Our Meeting	AB	Lon	13 Nov 33	Dec F-3742
Fare Thee Well	Lew Stone ahb	Lon	25 Jul 34	Dec F-5130
Farmyard Symphony, The	Billy Hill and his Boys	Lon	18 Dec 30	Dec F-2172
Ferry Boat Serenade, The	Al Bowlly and Jimmy Mesene	Lon	6 Dec 40	HMV BD-892
Fiesta	NMDO	Lon	28 Apr 31	HMV B-6010
Fiesta	Roy Fox ahb	Lon	5 May 31	Dec F-2341

Title	Artiste	Place	Date	Original Issue
Flowers For Madam	Ray Noble aho	NY	9 Mar 35	HMV BD-213*, Vic 24865*
Flowers For Madam	Ray Noble aho	NY	– – – – 35	Air Aircheck 2+ RT
Foolish Facts	Tuff Guys	Lon	8 Dec 31	EBR 1586
Foolish Facts	AB and the Radio Rhythm Five	Lon	9 Dec 31	EBW 5440
For You Alone	Ray Noble aho	Lon	16 May 33	HMV rejected
Frankie and Johnny	Al Bowlly and Ella Logan	Lon	24 Nov 30	Dec F-2206
Freckle Face, You're Beautiful	Ray Noble aho	Lon	24 Aug 34	HMV B-6512
Free And Easy, The	Blue Jays (Duet LA)	Lon	1 Dec 30	EBW 5202
Frog On The Water Lily	Lew Stone ahb	Lon	3 Oct 38	Dec F-6812*
Frog On The Water Lily	Lew Stone ahb	Lon	8 Oct 38	AC
From Me To You	Lew Stone ahb	Lon	18 Oct 33	Dec F-3716
Georgia's Gotta Moon	Lew Stone ahb	Lon	28 Nov 38	Dec F-6891*
Getting Sentimental	Roy Fox ahb	Lon	4 May 32	Dec F-2963
Girl In The Alice Blue Gown, The	Lew Stone ahb	Lon	4 Feb 38	Dec F-6607*
Girl In The Upstairs Flat, The	Felix Mendelssohn aho	Lon	1 Jul 38	Dec F-6726*
Girl Who Thought . . ., The (Parts 1 and 2)	Lew Stone and the Mons Band	Lon	9 Dec 32	Dec F-3324
Give Me A Tune	Ray Noble and the NMDO	Lon	7 Apr 32	HMV B-6182
Give Me Back My Heart	Night Club Kings	Lon	17 Jul 30	HMV rejected
Give Me My Ranch	AB acc orc dir Ronnie Munro	Lon	21 Dec 39	HMV BD-805
Glorious Devon	AB acc George Scott-Wood (p)	Lon	21 Dec 32	Dec F-3369
Go Home And Tell Your Mother	Edgar Adeler's Haw Pla (duet LA)	Lon	– – Nov 30	Sterno 604
Go Home And Tell Your Mother (unconfirmed)	Harry Hudson's Melody Men (duet LA)	Lon	– – Nov 30	EBR 1436
Goin' To Heaven On A Mule	Bohemians dir Walter Goehr	Lon	18 Apr 34	Col DX-583
Golden Gates Of Paradise, The	Linn Milford and his Haw Sing	Lon	2 Jul 30	Reg MR-128
Golden Gates Of Paradise, The	Hawaiian Quartet	Lon	24 Sep 30	Dec F-1991

Title	Artiste	Place	Date	Original Issue
Gone Forever	Roy Fox ahb	Lon	10 Jun 32	Dec F-3029
Goodbye To All That	Hawaiian Quartet (duet LA)	Lon	9 Sep 30	Dec rejected
Goodbye To All That	Honolulu Quartet (duet LA)	Lon	24 Sep 30	Dec F-1958
Good Evening	Arthur Lally aho (as Buddy Lewis aho on Pan; as Jack Holmes aho on May)	Lon	1 Jun 32	Dec F-3067, Pan 25240, May G-2170
Good Evening	Ray Noble and the NMDO	Lon	8 Jun 32	HMV B-6193
Goodnight	Rolando's Salon Orc	Lon	––Jul 31	EBW 5361
Goodnight, Angel	AB acc George Scott-Wood (pipe organ)	Lon	25 May 38	HMV BD-565
Goodnight, But Not Goodbye	AB	Lon	20 Apr 33	Dec F-3547
Goodnight, Little Girl Of My Dreams	Ray Noble aho	Lon	27 Oct 33	HMV B-6413
Goodnight, Moon	Roy Fox ahb	Lon	7 Mar 32	Dec F-2867
Goodnight, Sweetheart	NMDO	Lon	19 Feb 31	HMV B-5984, Vic 25016
Goodnight, Sweetheart	Novelty Orc	Lon	9 Mar 31	HMV B-3825
Goodnight, Sweetheart	Jack Leon ahb	Lon	––Jun 31	Pic 787, Oct 617
Goodnight, Sweetheart	New Mayfair Orc	Lon	26 Jun 31	HMV B-3907
Goodnight, Sweetheart	Ray Noble and his London Orc 'Ray Noble Medley'	Lon	24 Aug 36	HMV C-2872*, Vic 36194*
Goodnight, Vienna	Roy Fox ahb	Lon	22 Mar 32	Dec F-2889, Brun 6375
Goodnight, Vienna	Durium Dance Band	Lon	1 Apr 32	Durium En-9
Goodnight, Vienna	Ray Noble and the NMDO	Lon	7 Apr 32	HMV B-6172, Vic 24064
Goodnight Waltz, The	Scott-Wood Accordion Quartet	Lon	3 Apr 33	Parl R-1506
Goopy Geer	Masqueraders	Lon	24 Mar 32	Col CB-442
Gosh! I Must Be Falling In Love	Lew Stone ahb	Lon	15 Feb 34	Dec F-3884
Got A Date With An Angel	NMDO	Lon	14 Nov 31	HMV B-6098, Vic 22953
Got A Date With An Angel	Howard Godfrey and his Waldorfians, as Percy Chandler ahb on May	Lon	––Nov 31	Pic 855, Oct 133, May G-2062

138

Title	Artiste	Place	Date	Original Issue
Got A Date With An Angel (unconfirmed)	Rolando and his Blue Salon Orc (as a member of a vocal group)	Lon	–– Oct 31	EBW 5396
Grandma Said	Geraldo aho	Lon	3 Feb 39	HMV BD-5457*
Grandma Said	Geraldo aho	Lon	–– –– 39	Hal Hal-14 + RT
Granny's Photo Album	Masqueraders	Lon	18 Feb 32	Col CB-434
Great Big Bunch Of You, A	Savoy Hotel Orpheans	Lon	18 Jul 32	Col CB-482
Great Day	Alfredo ahb (duet LA)	Lon	17 Oct 30	EBW 5187
Grinzing	Ray Noble aho	Lon	24 Aug 34	HMV B-6519, Vic 24771
Guilty	NMDO	Lon	14 Nov 31	HMV B-6097
Guilty	Roy Fox ahb	Lon	2 Dec 31	Dec F-2716
Gypsy Dream Rose	Linn Milford and his Haw Pla	Lon	7 Mar '30	Reg rejected
Gypsy Dream Rose	Honolulu Serenaders (as Hawaiian Octet on Cel)	Lon	–– Mar 30	Dom C-319, Cel 4390
Gypsy Fiddles	Ray Noble aho	Lon	16 Jun 33	HMV B-6367
Half Moon On The Hudson	Al Bowlly aho	NY	3 Dec 37	HMV BD-5363,* BB B-7317
Hallelujah	Arthur Briggs' Sav Syn Orc	Ber	–– Oct 27	DG/Pol 21034
Hand In Hand	Ray Noble aho	Lon	9 Nov 33	HMV B-6423
Hand In Hand (a different song to the one above)	Lew Stone ahb	Lon	3 May 34	Dec F-3985*
Hang Out The Stars In Indiana	NMDO	Lon	25 Aug 31	HMV B-6058, Vic 24357
Hang Out The Stars In Indiana	Blue Jays	Lon	–– Sep 31	EBR 1556
Happy	Ray Noble aho	Lon	6 Jul 34	HMV B-6507
Happy And Contented	Ray Noble aho (with Eve Becke)	Lon	12 Oct 33	HMV B-6407
Happy Days Are Here Again	Brooklyn Broadcasters	Lon	–– Mar 30	Dom C-303
Happy Feet	Harry Hudson's Melody Men (duet LA)	Lon	–– Sep 30	EBW 5160
Happy-Go-Lucky You (And Broken Hearted Me)	AB	Lon	7 Sep 32	Dec F-3145

Title	Artiste	Place	Date	Original Issue
Happy-Go-Lucky You (And Broken Hearted Me)	AB 'OK Decca'	Lon	21 Oct 32	Dec K-684
Have A Heart	Ray Noble aho	Lon	1 Feb 34	HMV B-6459
Have You Ever Been In Heaven	Lew Stone ahb	Lon	21 Mar 38	Dec F-6641*
Have You Ever Been Lonely	Ray Noble aho	Lon	7 Feb 33	HMV B-6319, Vic 24278
Hawaiian Stars Are Gleaming	Len Fillis and his Novelty Orc (duet LA)	Lon	6 May 31	Col DB-516
Headin' For Hollywood	Hawaiian Serenaders	Lon	13 Nov 30	Victory 303
Heartaches	Sid Phillips and his Melodians	Lon	–– Aug 31	EBW 5358
Heart And Soul	Geraldo aho	Lon	11 Nov 38	HMV BD-5427*
Hello, Mike	Arthur Lally aho	Lon	29 Sep 32	Dec F-3187
Henry's Made A Lady Out Of Lizzie (unconfirmed)	Billy Bartholomew's Delphians	Ber	–– May 28	DG/Pol 21654
Here In My Heart	Linn Milford and his Haw Pla (duet LA)	Lon	19 Sep 30	Reg MR-187
Here Lies Love	Ray Noble aho	Lon	8 Dec 32	HMV B-6283
He's My Secret Passion – see 'She's My Secret Passion				
Hey Gypsy, Play Gypsy	AB acc orc dir Ronnie Munro	Lon	11 May 39	HMV BD-709
Hiawatha's Lullaby	Ray Noble aho	Lon	16 May 33	HMV B-6359
Hoe Gaan Dit? (in Taal dialect)	AB as Jannie Viljoen acc Claude Ivy (p)	Lon	13 Oct 30	Dec rejected
Hold My Hand	Ray Noble and the NMDO	Lon	1 Dec 31	HMV B-6112, Vic 24034
Hold My Hand	Jock McDermott ahb	Lon	5 Jan 32	EBW 5458
Hold My Hand (a different song to the one above)	Ray Noble aho	Lon	28 Jun 34	HMV B-6499
Homestead – see 'Woorhuis'				
Hometown	Ronnie Munro aho	Lon	17 Jul 37	HMV BD-5248, BB B-7334
Honeymoon Chimes	Linn Milford and his Haw Pla	Lon	15 May 29	Reg G-9362
Honeymoon Lane	NMDO	Lon	25 Aug 31	HMV B-6058

Title	Artiste	Place	Date	Original Issue
Honeymoon Lane	Radio Rhythm Boys	Lon	–– Sep 31	EBR 1551
How Could I Be Lonely?	NMDO	Lon	20 Nov 30	HMV B-5940, Vic 24752
How Could We Be Wrong?	Ray Noble aho	Lon	18 Sep 33	HMV B-6396, Vic 24872
How Could We Be Wrong?	Lew Stone ahb	Lon	3 Nov 33	Dec F-3734
How Do You Do? – see 'Hoe Gaan Dit?'				
How'm I Doin'?	Roy Fox ahb (as a member of a chorus)	Lon	23 Sep 32	Dec F-3198
Hurt	Palm Beach Hawaiians	Lon	23 Jan 31	Dec F-2317
Hurt	Roy Fox ahb	Lon	28 Jan 31	Dec F-2239
Hustling And Bustling For Baby	Ray Noble aho	Lon	16 Mar 33	HMV B-6331
Hymns My Mother Used To Sing, The	Linn Milford and his Haw Sing	Lon	2 Jul 30	Reg MR-197
I Built A Dream One Day	Ray Noble aho	NY	9 Dec 35	Vic 25200*
(I Can Dream), Can't I?	Al Bowlly aho	NY	3 Dec 37	HMV BD-5363*, BB B-7332*
I Can't Do Without You	Radio Rhythm Boys (with chorus)	Lon	–– Sep 31	EBR 1551
I Can't Get Mississippi Off My Mind	Billy Cotton ahb	Lon	1 Dec 31	Reg MR-463
I Can't Give You Anything But Love	Ray Noble aho	NY	–– –– 35	RT
I Can't Write The Words	Lew Stone and the Mons Band	Lon	11 Nov 32	Dec rejected
I Can't Write The Words	Lew Stone and the Mons Band	Lon	16 Nov 32	Dec F-3270*, May G-277
Ich Liebe Dich, My Dear	Lew Stone and the Mons Band	Lon	23 Dec 32	Dec F-3372*
I Double Dare You	Lew Stone ahb	Lon	4 Feb 38	Dec F-6606*
I'd Rather Be A Beggar With You	NMDO	Lon	11 Jun 31	HMV B-6040
I'd Rather Be A Beggar With You	Roy Fox ahb	Lon	31 Jul 31	Dec F-2438, F-2609*
I'd Rather Be A Beggar With You	AB	Lon	2 Sep 31	Dec F-2485
If Anything Happened To You	Fred Elizalde's Rhythmicians	Lon	4 Dec 29	Met 1241, Oct 367
If Anything Happened To You (a different song to the one above)	Lew Stone ahb	Lon	–– –– 31	FS

Title	Artiste	Place	Date	Original Issue
If Anything Happened To You	Rhythm Maniacs (Roy Fox ahb)	Lon	28 Jan 32	Dec F-3086
If Ever A Heart Was In The Right Place	Geraldo aho	Lon	10 Jan 39	HMV BD-5448*
If I Didn't Have You	Roy Fox ahb	Lon	30 Dec 31	Dec F-2763
If I Had A Million Dollars	AB acc orc dir Victor Young	NY	30 Oct 34	Dec F-5326, 293
If I Had You	Fred Elizalde and his Music	Lon	21 Nov 28	Brun 3948
If I Have To Go On Without You	Roy Fox ahb	Lon	7 Mar 32	Dec F-2866
I Found A Million Dollar Baby	Roy Fox ahb	Lon	16 Oct 31	Dec F-2610
I Found You	Roy Fox ahb	Lon	21 Jul 31	Dec F-2404*
If You'll Say 'Yes', Cherie	Ray Noble aho	Lon	13 Jul 33	HMV B-6379
If You Love Me	Ray Noble aho	NY	23 Jan 36	HMV BD-5046*, Vic 25240*
If You Were Only Mine	Roy Fox ahb	Lon	9 Sep 32	Dec F-3151
I Got Rhythm	Roy Fox ahb	Lon	19 May 32	Dec F-3014
I Haven't Time To Be A Millionaire	Al Bowlly and Jimmy Mesene	Lon	12 Sep 40	HMV BD-865
I Heard	Savoy Hotel Orpheans	Lon	18 Jul 32	Col CB-483
I Idolize My Baby's Eyes	New Cumberland Dance Orc	Lon	–– Jan 32	Film 378
I Lay Me Down To Sleep	Lew Stone and the Mons Band	Lon	7 Jun 33	Dec F-3603
I'll Be Good Because Of You	Novelty Orc	Lon	9 Mar 31	HMV B-3825
I'll Do My Best To Make You Happy	Ray Noble and the NMDO	Lon	8 Sep 32	HMV B-6245, Vic 24333
I'll Do My Best To Make You Happy	AB	Lon	19 Sep 32	Dec rejected
I'll Do My Best To Make You Happy	AB	Lon	7 Oct 32	Dec F-3194
I'll Follow You	AB acc George Scott-Wood (p)	Lon	15 Nov 32	Dec F-3304
I'll Forsake All Others	Ray Noble aho	NY	7 Dec 36	Lon HMG-5027+RT
I'll Keep You In My Heart Always	Jack Leon ahb	Lon	–– Jun 31	Pic 788
I'll Never Be The Same	Lew Stone and the Mons Band	Lon	2 Dec 32	Dec F-3314*
I'll Never Smile Again	Al Bowlly and Jimmy Mesene	Lon	12 Sep 40	HMV BD-865

Title	Artiste	Place	Date	Original Issue
I'll String Along With You	Ray Noble aho	Lon	28 Jun 34	HMV B-6503
I Love No One But You	John Abriani's Six	Ber	17 Jan 28	Hom 4-2514
I Love You Truly	Lew Stone ahb	Lon	3 May 34	Dec F-5003*
I Love You Truly	Ray Noble aho	Lon	31 May 34	HMV B-6492, Vic 24806
I Love You Truly	Ray Noble aho	NY	7 Dec 36	Lon HMG-5027+ RT
I'm A Hundred Per Cent In Love With You	Radio Melody Boys	Lon	–– Aug 31	EBR 1535
I'm Alone In Athlone	AB acc Fred Bird (vn); Edgar Adeler (p)	Ber	23 Sep 27	Hom 4-2418
I'm Coming, Virginia	Arthur Briggs' Sav Syn Orc	Ber	–– Oct 27	DG/Pol 21125
I'm Forever Thinking Of You – see 'Ek Dink Altyd Aan Jou'				
I'm For You A Hundred Per Cent	Roy Fox ahb	Lon	13 Apr 32	Dec F-2923
I'm Getting Sentimental Over You	AB	Lon	26 Jul 33	Dec F-3638
I'm Glad I Waited	NMDO	Lon	19 Feb 31	HMV B-5983
I'm Glad I Waited	Roy Fox ahb (as member of trio)	Lon	13 Mar 31	Dec F-2291
I'm Glad I Waited	Deauville Dance Band	Lon	–– Jun 31	EBW 5315
I'm Gonna Get You	Roy Fox ahb	Lon	1 Jun 31	Dec F-2351*
I'm Gonna Sit Right Down And Write Myself A Letter	AB ('Al Bowlly Remembers')	Lon	11 Nov 38	Dec F-6916
I'm In Love With Vienna	Geraldo aho	Lon	10 Jan 39	HMV BD-5449*
I Miss You In The Morning	AB acc orc dir Ronnie Munro	Lon	14 Feb 39	HMV BD-673
I Miss You In The Morning	Geraldo aho	Lon	4 Apr 39	HMV BD-5473
I'm Looking For A Bluebird (To Chase My Blues Away)	AB	Ber	22 Sep 27	Hom 4-2414
I'm Madly In Love With You	Reginald Williams and his Futurists	Lon	8 Feb 39	Col FB-2167
I'm Misunderstood	Ray Noble aho	NY	24 Apr 35	JA JA-22+ RT
I'm One Of The Lads Of Valencia	Ray Noble aho (with chorus)	Lon	25 Apr 33	HMV B-6344

Title	Artiste	Place	Date	Original Issue
I'm Playing With Fire	Jack Jackson aho	Lon	24 Feb 33	HMV B-6322
I'm Saving The Last Waltz For You	Felix Mendelssohn aho	Lon	1 Jul 38	Dec F-6727*
I'm Sorry I Didn't Say I'm Sorry	Lew Stone ahb	Lon	12 Aug 38	Dec F-6744*
I'm Sorry, Sally	Fred Elizalde and his Music	Lon	––Dec 28	Brun 206
I'm So Used To You Now	Roy Fox ahb	Lon	1 Jun 31	Dec F-2352*
I'm So Used To You Now	AB acc Claude Ivy (p)	Lon	10 Jun 31	Dec F-2366
I'm So Used To You Now	Jack Leon ahb	Lon	––Jun 31	Pic 796
I'm Stepping Out With A Memory, Tonight	Al Bowlly and Jimmy Mesene	Lon	12 Sep 40	HMV BD-865
I'm Telling The World She's Mine	NMDO	Lon	20 Nov 30	HMV B-5940, Vic 24752
I'm The Fellow Who Loves You	Ray Noble aho (with the Freshmen)	NY	14 Nov 35	Vic 25190*
I'm Thru With Love	Deauville Dance Band	Lon	––Sep 31	EBR 1558
I'm Walking On Air	Arthur Briggs' Sav Syn Orc	Ber	––Oct 27	DG/Pol 21131
In A Blue And Pensive Mood	AB acc orc dir Ray Noble	NY	12 Jan 35	HMV B-8302, BD-230, Vic 24849
In A Little Gypsy Tea Room	Ray Noble aho	NY	13 May 35	Lon HMG-5019+ RT
In A Little Spanish Town	Fred Bird, The Salon Symphonic Jazz Band	Ber	12 Sep 27	Hom 4-2389
In A Little Toy Sailboat	Geraldo aho	Lon	14 Oct 38	HMV BD-5421*
In An Old Churchyard	Linn Milford and his Haw Pla	Lon	17 Dec 30	Reg MR-337
In A Shelter From A Shower	Lew Stone ahb	Lon	16 Mar 34	Dec F-3942
In Die Droomvallei (in Taal dialect)	AB as Jannie Viljoen acc Claude Ivy (p)	Lon	13 Oct 30	Dec rejected
I Never Had A Chance	Ray Noble aho	Lon	18 Jul 34	HMV B-6509
I Never Had A Chance	Lew Stone ahb	Lon	25 Jul 34	Dec F-5131*
I Never Had A Chance	Ray Noble aho	NY	–– –– 35	Air Aircheck 2+ RT
In London On A Night Like This	Lew Stone ahb	Lon	–– –– 31	FS

Title	Artiste	Place	Date	Original Issue
In London On A Night Like This	Rhythm Maniacs (Roy Fox ahb)	Lon	28 Jan 32	Dec F-3086
In My Little Red Book	Mantovani aho	Lon	4 Mar 38	Col FB-1925
In My Little Red Book	Lew Stone ahb	Lon	21 Mar 38	Dec F-6642*
In Santa Lucia	Lew Stone and the Mons Band	Lon	27 Jan 33	Dec F-3456
In Santa Margherita	Lew Stone ahb	Lon	21 Apr 38	Dec F-6663*
In The Moonlight	Linn Milford and his Haw Sing	Lon	24 Jan 30	Reg MR-28
In The Park In Paree	Lew Stone and the Mons Band	Lon	7 Jan 33	Dec F-3592
In The Still Of The Night	Lew Stone and the Mons Dance Orc	Lon	21 Oct 32	Dec rejected
In The Still Of The Night	Lew Stone and the Mons Dance Orc	Lon	31 Oct 32	Dec F-3234*
In The Still Of The Night (a different song to the one above)	New Mayfair Orc dir Ronnie Munro	Lon	14 Jan 38	HMV BD-502*
In The Still Of The Night	Maurice Winnick and his Sweet Music	Lon	20 Jan 38	Dec F-6605*
In The Valley Of Dreams – see 'In Die Droomvallei'				
I Offer You These Roses	Jack Leon ahb	Lon	– – Jun 31	Pic 799
I Only Want One Girl	Ray Noble aho	Lon	20 Jun 33	HMV B-6366
I Shall Still Keep Smiling Along	Ray Noble aho	Lon	16 May 33	HMV B-6359, Vic 24393
Is I In Love? I Is	Arthur Lally aho	Lon	23 Jul 32	Dec F-3066*
Isle Of Capri	AB acc Monia Liter (p)	Lon	21 Aug 34	Dec F-5188, Champion 40032
Isle Of Capri	Ray Noble aho	Lon	30 Aug 34	HMV B-6519, Vic 24771
Isn't It Heavenly	Lew Stone and the Mons Band	Lon	1 Aug 33	Dec F-3630
Isn't It Heavenly	The Bands That Matter (The massed bands of Ambrose, Roy Fox, Jack Hylton and Lew Stone)	Lon	25 Oct 33	Dec F-3723
Is That The Way To Treat A Sweetheart?	Geraldo aho	Lon	3 Dec 38	HMV BD-5438*
It All Depends On You	Arthur Briggs' Sav Syn Orc	Ber	– – Oct 27	DG/Pol 21124

145

Title	Artiste	Place	Date	Original Issue
It Happened In Monterey	AB acc John Watt's Songs from the Shows	Lon	7 Mar 32	Dec K-645
It Must Be True	Roy Fox ahb	Lon	1 Jun 31	Dec F-2351*
It's A Blue World	Macari aho	Lon	4 May 40	Reg rejected
It's All Forgotten Now	Ray Noble aho	Lon	11 Jul 34	HMV B-6509, Vic 24724
It's All Forgotten Now	AB acc Monia Liter (p)	Lon	16 Jul 34	Dec F-5121
It's A Long, Long Way To Your Heart	Sidney Lipton and his Grosvenor House Orc	Lon	13 Jan 38	Dec F-6608*
It's A Lovely Day Tomorrow	AB acc orc dir Billy Munn	Lon	15 Feb 40	HMV BD-828
It's Always Goodbye	Roy Fox ahb	Lon	10 Jun 32	Dec F-3028
It's Bad For Me	Ray Noble aho	Lon	19 Sep 33	HMV B-6396, Vic 24872
It's Great To Be In Love	Ray Noble and the NMDO	Lon	12 Feb 32	HMV B-6147, Vic 25232
It's Psychological	Lew Stone ahb	Lon	23 Mar 34	Dec DDV 5009/10+
It's Sunday Down In Carolina	Ray Noble aho	Lon	12 Jul 33	HMV B-6381
It's Time To Say Goodnight	Ray Noble aho	Lon	16 Feb 34	HMV B-6459
It's Time To Say Goodnight	Ray Noble aho	NY	9 Apr 35	RT
It's Within Your Power	Ray Noble aho	Lon	3 May 33	HMV B-6347
It Was A Lover And His Lass	Ken 'Snakehips' Johnson and his West Indian Orc (with the Henderson Twins)	Lon	24 Apr 40	HMV BD-5592*
It Was So Beautiful	AB	Lon	7 Sep 32	Dec F-3145
It Was So Beautiful	Monia Liter and the Ace of Hearts Orc	Lon	---- 38	Fan LP-40-140+ RT
I've Got To Pass Your House To Get To My House	Ray Noble aho	Lon	19 Sep 33	HMV rejected
I've Got To Sing A Torch Song	Ray Noble aho	Lon	5 Jul 33	HMV B-6375
I've Got You Under My Skin	Ray Noble aho	NY	25 Sep 36	HMV BD-5147*, Vic 25422*
I've Got You Under My Skin	Ray Noble aho	NY	---- 36	RT
I've Had My Moments	Lew Stone ahb	Lon	3 Aug 34	Dec F-5131

146

Title	Artiste	Place	Date	Original Issue
I Was True	Ray Noble and the NMDO (with chorus)	Lon	19 Dec 31	HMV B-6118
I Wished On The Moon	Ray Noble aho	NY	20 Jul 35	HMV BD-211*, Vic 25104*
I Wonder (unconfirmed)	Billy Bartholomew's Delphians	Ber	– – May 28	DG/Pol 21596
I Won't Tell A Soul	Lew Stone ahb	Lon	15 Aug 38	Dec F-6763*
Japanese Dream, A	Radio Melody Boys (duet LA)	Lon	1 Dec 30	EBW 5203
Jig Time	Roy Fox ahb	Lon	21 Jan 32	Dec F-2793
Judy	AB acc Monia Liter (p)	Lon	21 Aug 34	Dec F-5188, Champion 40032
June Time Is Love Time	NMDO	Lon	29 May 31	HMV B-6023
Junk Man Blues	Lew Stone and the Mons Band (with chorus)	Lon	29 Nov 32	Dec F-3313
Just A Dancing Sweetheart	NMDO	Lon	14 Aug 31	HMV B-6056
Just An Echo In The Valley	Ray Noble aho	Lon	12 Jan 33	HMV B-6305
Just Another Dream Of You	Roy Fox ahb	Lon	8 Aug 32	Dec F-3094
Just An Ugly Duckling	AB acc Claude Bampton (p)	Lon	– – – – 39	PR
Just Humming Along	Durium Dance Band	Lon	20 Apr 32	Durium EN-13
Just Imagine	Fred Elizalde and his Music	Lon	25 Jul 28	Brun 189
Just Let Me Look At You	Lew Stone ahb	Lon	12 Aug 38	Dec F-6745*
Just Once Again	John Abriani's Six	Ber	17 Jan 28	Hom 4-2188
Just One More Chance	Blue Jays	Lon	– – Sep 31	EBR 1556
Just One More Chance	Roy Fox ahb	Lon	2 Oct 31	Dec F-2580
Keeping Out Of Mischief Now	Savoy Hotel Orpheans	Lon	11 May 32	Col rejected
Keep Your Last Goodnight For Me	AB	Lon	7 Oct 32	Dec F-3218
Kicking The Gong Around	Roy Fox ahb	Lon	22 Feb 32	Dec F-2834
King Was In The Counting House, The	Masqueraders	Lon	24 Mar 32	Col CB-443
Kiss By Kiss	Masqueraders (with the Carlyle Cousins)	Lon	18 Feb 32	Col CB-429

Title	Artiste	Place	Date	Original Issue
Kiss By Kiss	Roy Fox ahb	Lon	7 Mar 32	Dec F-2867
Kiss Me Goodnight	Roy Fox ahb	Lon	2 Oct 31	Dec F-2581
Kiss Me Goodnight (a different song to the one above)	Maurice Winnick and his Sweet Music	Lon	29 Dec 37	Dec F-6591*
Kiss Waltz, The	Waikiki Serenaders (duet LA)	Lon	–– Nov 30	Bdcst 643
Kleine Maat (in Afrikaans)	AB	Hay	14 Jul 30	HMV FJ-97
Koppa-Ka-Banna	Roy Fox ahb	Lon	1 Apr 31	Dec F-2315
Lady Of Madrid	Ray Noble aho	Lon	18 Jul 34	HMV B-6510, Vic 24724
Lady Of Spain	NMDO (as London Mayfair Orc on Victors)	Lon	24 Mar 31	HMV B-5999, Vic 22774, Vic 24499
Lady Of Spain	Roy Fox ahb	Lon	25 Mar 31	Dec F-2279
Lady Of Spain	Len Fillis and his Novelty Orc (duet LA)	Lon	6 May 31	Col DB-549
Lady, Play Your Mandoline	Roy Fox ahb	Lon	24 Jan 31	Dec F-2220
Land Of The Might-Have-Been	Edgar Adeler's Haw Pla	Lon	–– Mar 30	Sterno 594, Solex 6
Language Of Love, The	Lew Stone and the Mons Band	Lon	7 Jun 33	Dec F-3603
Last Night I Dreamed You Kissed Me	Linn Milford and his Haw Sing with Les Allen	Lon	5 Nov 29	Reg G-9442
Laughing At The Rain	Roy Fox ahb	Lon	21 Apr 31	Dec F-2328
Lay My Head Beneath A Rose	Linn Milford and his Haw Sing	Lon	5 Nov 29	Reg G-9422
Lazy Day	NMDO	Lon	11 Jun 31	HMV B-6031
Lazy Day	Roy Fox ahb	Lon	16 Jun 31	Dec F-2396*
Lazy Lou'siana Moon	Edgar Adeler's Haw Pla	Lon	–– Mar 30	Sterno 406
Learn To Croon	AB	Lon	26 Jul 33	Dec F-3627
Leave The Rest To Nature	Roy Fox ahb	Lon	1 Jun 31	Dec F-2352*
Leave The Rest To Nature	AB acc Claude Ivy (p)	Lon	10 Jun 31	Dec F-2366
Leave The Rest To Nature	Jack Leon ahb	Lon	–– Jun 31	Pic 796
Let Bygones Be Bygones	Jack Jackson aho	Lon	24 Feb 33	HMV B-6330
Let Me Give My Happiness To You	Ray Noble aho	Lon	16 Mar 33	HMV B-6332

Title	Artiste	Place	Date	Original Issue
Let Me Give My Happiness To You	Lew Stone and the Mons Band	Lon	5 Apr 33	Dec F-3534
Le Touquet	Ronnie Munro aho	Lon	17 Jul 37	HMV BD-5242*
Let's All Sing Like The Birdies Sing	Lew Stone and the Mons Band	Lon	9 Dec 32	Dec F-3345
Let's Call A Heart A Heart	Ray Noble aho	NY	25 Sep 36	Vic 25428*
Let's Face The Music And Dance	Ray Noble aho	NY	23 Jan 36	HMV BD-5047*, Vic 25241*
Let's Face The Music And Dance	Ray Noble aho	NY	9 Feb 36	Radiola 3 MR-1+ RT
Let's Get Friendly	Radio Rhythm Boys	Lon	--Jun 31	EBR 1508
Let's Put Our Heads Together	Ray Noble aho	NY	----36	RT
Let's Put Out The Lights And Go To Sleep	Lew Stone and the Mons Band (with Mary Charles)	Lon	11 Nov 32	Dec rejected
Let's Put Out The Lights And Go To Sleep	Lew Stone and the Mons Band (with Mary Charles)	Lon	16 Nov 32	Dec F-3270*
Letter To My Mother, A (in Yiddish)	Lew Stone and the Mons Band	Lon	10 Jan 33	Dec F-3428
Letter To My Mother, A (in Yiddish)	Lew Stone and the Mons Band	Lon	27 Jan 33	Dec F-3428
Letter To My Mother, A	Ray Noble aho	Lon	31 Jan 33	HMV B-6317, Vic 24308
Let Yourself Go	Ray Noble aho (with the Freshmen)	NY	23 Jan 36	HMV BD-5047*, Vic 25241
Let Yourself Go	Ray Noble aho	NY	9 Feb 36	Radiola 3 MR-1+ RT
Lies	Deauville Dance Band	Lon	--Nov 31	EBR 1584
Life Is A Song	Ray Noble aho	NY	1 May 35	JA JA-22+ RT
Life Is Just A Bowl Of Cherries	Roy Fox ahb	Lon	5 Nov 31	Dec F-2682
Life Is Just A Bowl Of Cherries	New Cumberland Dance Orc	Lon	--Jan 32	Film 379
Life Is Meant For Love	Waldorfians dir Howard Godfrey	Lon	--Jun 30	Pic 781, Oct 613
Lights Of Paris	NMDO	Lon	29 May 31	HMV B-6023, Vic 24004
Lights Of Paris	Jack Leon ahb	Lon	--Jun 31	Pic 782, Oct 614

Title	Artiste	Place	Date	Original Issue
Linda	Savoy Hotel Orpheans	Lon	31 Oct 31	Col CB-377
Linda	Blue Jays	Lon	–– Nov 31	EBR 1585
Listen To The German Band	Debroy Somers ahb	Lon	20 Sep 32	Col CB-508
Little Drummer Boy	Lew Stone ahb	Lon	4 Feb 38	Dec F-6607*
Little Dutch Mill	AB acc Monia Liter (p)	Lon	9 Apr 34	Dec F-3956
Little Dutch Mill	Ray Noble aho	Lon	21 Apr 34	HMV B-6482
Little Girl, A Little Boy, A Little Moon, A (unconfirmed)	Billy Bartholomew's Delphians	Ber	–– May 28	DG/Pol 21605
Little Lady Make Believe	Lew Stone ahb	Lon	12 Aug 38	Dec F-6744*
Little Lady Make Believe	AB acc Felix Mendelssohn aho 'Singers on Parade'	Lon	10 Oct 38	Dec F-6831
Little Love Song, A	Blue Jays (Duet LA)	Lon	30 Dec 30	EBR 1448
Little Love Song, A	Marius B. Winter and his Dance Orc	Lon	–– Jan 31	Bdcst 3004
Little Man, You've Had A Busy Day	Ray Noble aho	Lon	31 May 34	HMV B-6491
Little Nell	Lew Stone and the Mons Band	Lon	10 Jan 33	Dec F-3394
Little Old Lady	Ray Noble aho	NY	16 Oct 36	HMV BD-5287*, Vic 25448*
Little Old Lady	Ray Noble aho	NY	7 Dec 36	Lon HMG-5019+ RT
Little Pal – see 'Kleine Maat'				
Little Rain Must Fall, A	AB acc orc dir Ronnie Munro	Lon	7 Mar 40	HMV BD-827
Little Street Where Old Friends Meet, A	Ray Noble aho	Lon	12 Jan 33	HMV B-6305
Little Valley In The Mountains	Ray Noble aho	Lon	18 Jul 34	HMV B-6512
Little White Gardenia, A	AB acc orc dir Ray Noble	NY	12 Jan 35	HMV B-8302, BD-230, Vic 24855
Little White House, The	Arthur Briggs' Sav Syn Orc	Ber	–– Oct 27	DG/Pol 21135
Living In Clover	Roy Fox ahb	Lon	22 Mar 32	Dec F-2889, Brun 6375
Living In Clover	Ray Noble and the NMDO	Lon	7 Apr 32	HMV B-6172, Vic 24064

150

Title	Artiste	Place	Date	Original Issue
Living In The Sunlight, Loving In The Moonlight	Alfredo ahb (duet LA)	Lon	17 Oct 30	EBW 5188
Lonely	AB acc orc dir Ronnie Munro	Lon	14 Feb 39	HMV BD-666
Lonely Feet	Lew Stone ahb	Lon	25 Apr 34	Dec F-3985*
Lonely Little Vagabond	Phantom Players	Lon	3 Nov 30	Dec F-2144
Lonely Little Vagabond	Earl Melville and his Hawaiians	Lon	–– Nov 30	Pic 649
Lonesome Road, The (in Afrikaans)	AB	Hay	14 Jul 30	HMV FJ-97
Lonesome Trail Ain't Lonesome Anymore, The	Sidney Lipton and his Grosvenor House Orc	Lon	13 Jan 38	Dec F-6608*
Longer That You Linger In Virginia, The	Roy Fox ahb	Lon	30 Dec 31	Dec F-2760
Looking For A Little Bit Of Blue	Lew Stone ahb	Lon	3 Aug 34	Dec F-5270
Looking For You	Roy Fox ahb	Lon	2 Oct 31	Dec F-2574
Looking For You	Howard Godfrey and his Waldorfians	Lon	–– Nov 31	Pic 849, Oct 133
Looking On The Bright Side Of Life	Ray Noble and the NMDO	Lon	1 Sep 32	HMV B-6237, Vic 24212
Looking On The Bright Side (same song as the one above)	Arthur Lally aho (as Jack Holmes aho on Mayfair)	Lon	29 Sep 32	Pan 25303*, May G-2203
Look In The Looking Glass	Roy Fox ahb	Lon	16 Oct 31	Dec F-2610
Look What You've Done	Ray Noble aho	Lon	7 Feb 33	HMV B-6321
Louisiana Hayride	Lew Stone ahb	Lon	9 Jan 34	Dec F-3840
Lovable	Roy Fox ahb	Lon	4 May 32	Dec F-2963
Love Birds Are Better Than Bluebirds	Hawaiian Serenaders	Lon	13 Nov 30	Victory 298
Love For Sale	Roy Fox ahb	Lon	21 Jul 31	Dec F-2404
Love In Bloom	Lew Stone ahb	Lon	3 Aug 34	Dec F-5158
Love Is The Sweetest Thing	Ray Noble and the NMDO	Lon	8 Sep 32	HMV B-6245, Vic 24333
Love Is The Sweetest Thing	AB	Lon	19 Sep 32	Dec rejected
Love Is The Sweetest Thing	AB	Lon	7 Oct 32	Dec F-3194
Love Is The Sweetest Thing	Ray Noble aho 'Ray Noble Medley'	NY	13 May 35	Lon HMG-5019+ RT

Title	Artiste	Place	Date	Original Issue
Love Locked Out	Ray Noble aho	Lon	12 Oct 33	HMV B-6407, Vic 24485
Love Locked Out	AB acc orc dir Carroll Gibbons	Lon	16 Oct 33	Dec F-3695
Love Made A Gypsy Out Of Me	Linn Milford and his Haw Sing	Lon	24 Jan 30	Reg rejected
Love Never Dies	Hawaiian Serenaders	Lon	13 Nov 30	Victory 297
Lover, Come Back To Me	AB	Lon	13 Nov 33	Dec F-3742
Lover, Come Back To Me	AB ('Al Bowlly Remembers')	Lon	11 Nov 38	Dec F-6916
Love Tales	Ray Noble aho	Lon	7 Feb 33	HMV B-6319, Vic 24278
Love, (Wonderful Love)	Ray Noble aho	Lon	30 Aug 34	HMV B-6514
Love, You Funny Thing	Roy Fox ahb	Lon	4 May 32	Dec F-2964
Lullaby In Blue	Lew Stone ahb	Lon	15 Feb 34	Dec F-3884
Lullaby Land	Hawaiian Serenaders	Lon	13 Nov 30	Victory 301
Lullaby Of Broadway	Ray Noble aho	NY	13 May 35	Lon HMG-5019+ RT
Lullaby Of The Leaves	Roy Fox ahb (with trio)	Lon	10 Jun 32	Dec F-3029
Lying In The Hay	Lew Stone and the Mons Band	Lon	23 Dec 32	Dec F-3372
Lying In The Hay	Ray Noble aho	Lon	12 Jan 33	HMV B-6306, Vic 24297
Mademoiselle	Ray Noble aho	Lon	18 Sep 33	HMV B-6394, Vic 24624
Madonna Mine	AB acc Monia Liter (p)	Lon	16 Jul 34	Dec F-5121
Make Believe Island	Al Bowlly and Jimmy Mesene	Lon	18 Jul 40	HMV BD-857
Make Love With A Guitar	Al Bowlly and Jimmy Mesene	Lon	18 Jul 40	HMV BD-857
Make Yourself A Happiness Pie	NMDO	Lon	31 Dec 30	HMV B-5957
Makin' Wickey-Wackey Down In Waikiki	Radio Rhythm Boys	Lon	–– Feb 31	EBR 1489
Makin' Wickey-Wackey Down In Waikiki	NMDO	Lon	19 Feb 31	HMV B-5989

152

Title	Artiste	Place	Date	Original Issue
Mama Inez	Blue Jays	Lon	–– Aug 31	EBR 1541
Mama, I Wanna Make Rhythm	Lew Stone ahb	Lon	21 Apr 38	Dec F-6664*
Man And His Dream, A	AB acc orc dir Ronnie Munro	Lon	5 Oct 39	HMV BD-776
Marching Along Together	Ray Noble and the NMDO	Lon	11 Oct 32	HMV B-6249
Maria, My Own	AB	Lon	20 Apr 33	Dec F-3560
Maria, My Own	AB acc George Scott-Wood (pipe organ)	Lon	25 May 38	HMV rejected
Marie	AB acc orc dir Ronnie Munro	Lon	4 Jan 38	HMV BD-493
Marta	Roy Fox ahb	Lon	20 Jul 32	Dec rejected
Marta	Roy Fox ahb	Lon	8 Aug 32	Dec F-3093
Marta	AB acc George Scott-Wood (pipe organ)	Lon	25 May 38	HMV rejected
Mauna Loa	Lew Stone ahb	Lon	23 Mar 34	Dec F-3952
Maybe I Love You Too Much	Ray Noble aho	Lon	3 May 33	HMV B-6347
Maybe It's Love	Roy Fox ahb	Lon	9 Feb 31	Dec F-2240
Maybe It's Love	Radio Melody Boys (duet LA)	Lon	–– Mar 31	EBR 1478
Maybe I Will	Arthur Briggs' Sav Syn Orc	Ber	–– Oct 27	DG/Pol 21132
Me And My Shadow	Arthur Briggs' Sav Syn Orc	Ber	–– Oct 27	DG/Pol 21130
Mediterranean Madness	Lew Stone and the Mons Band	Lon	27 Jan 33	Dec F-3455, 656
Meet Me Tonight In The Cowshed	Ray Noble and the NMDO (with Leonard Henry)	Lon	8 Jan 32	HMV B-6130
Melody In Spring	Lew Stone ahb	Lon	24 Apr 34	Dec F-3979*
Memories Of You	Roy Fox ahb	Lon	5 Jan 31	Dec F-2194
Midnight, The Stars And You	Ray Noble aho	Lon	16 Feb 34	HMV B-6461, Vic 24700
Million Dreams, A	AB acc George Scott-Wood (p)	Lon	15 Nov 32	Dec F-3304
Minnaarslaan (in Taal Dialect)	AB as Jannie Viljoen acc Claude Ivy (p)	Lon	13 Oct 30	Dec rejected
Minnie The Moocher	Roy Fox ahb (with Lew Stone and Bill Harty)	Lon	22 Feb 32	Dec F-2834
Minnie The Moocher	Lew Stone ahb (with Tiny Winters and Bill Harty) 'Lew Stone Favourites'	Lon	1 Dec 33	Dec K-715

Title	Artiste	Place	Date	Original Issue
Minnie The Moocher	Lew Stone ahb (with Tiny Winters and Bill Harty) 'Lew Stone Favourites	Lon	12 Dec 33	AC
Minnie The Moocher's Wedding Day	Roy Fox ahb	Lon	20 Jul 32	Dec F-3063
Misery Farm	Fred Elizalde and his Music	Lon	–– Dec 28	Brun 206
Miss Elizabeth Brown	Waldorfians dir Howard Godfrey (as Basil Winston ahb on Empire, as Fifth Avenue Dance Orc on Mayfair)	Lon	–– Jun 31	Pic 780, Empire E-12, May M1–2019
Missouri Waltz	Roy Fox ahb	Lon	24 Jan 31	Dec F-2233
Moment I Saw You, The	Ray Noble aho	Lon	27 Feb 33	HMV B-6325, Vic 24610, 25313
Mona Lisa	Jock McDermott ahb	Lon	5 Jan 32	EBW 5458
Moon	Roy Fox ahb	Lon	23 Sep 32	Dec F-3198
Moon Country	Ray Noble aho	Lon	6 Jul 34	HMV B-6507
Moonlight In Hilo	Ray Noble aho	NY	19 Mar 36	Vic 25282*
Moonlight On The Colorado	Ferrachini's Hawaiian Band (duet LA)	Lon	–– Nov 30	Bdcst 2605, 3018
Moonlight On The Highway	Lew Stone ahb	Lon	21 Mar 38	Dec F-6641*
Moon Love	AB acc orc dir Ronnie Munro	Lon	5 Oct 39	HMV BD-762
Moonstruck	AB	Lon	26 Jul 33	Dec F-3627
Muddy Water	AB	Ber	22 Sep 27	Hom 4-2411
Music, Maestro, Please	Lew Stone ahb	Lon	15 Aug 38	Dec F-6777*
Must It End Like This	Ray Noble and the NMDO	Lon	8 Jan 32	HMV B-6130
My Angel Mother	Linn Milford and his Haw Sing	Lon	2 Jul 30	Reg MR-128
My Baby Just Cares For Me	Duet with Elsie Carlisle acc John Watt's Songs from the Shows	Lon	7 Mar 32	Dec K-645
My Bluebird Was Caught In The Rain	Ferrachini's Hawaiian Band	Lon	–– Jan 31	Bdcst 3008
My Blue Heaven	John Abriani's Six	Ber	17 Jan 28	Hom 4-2511*, 4-2611
My Canary Has Circles Under His	Waldorfians dir Howard Godfrey (as	Lon	–– Jun 30	Pic 780, Simcha

154

Title	Artiste	Place	Date	Original Issue
Eyes	Fifth Avenue Syncopaters on Mayfair, as Cosmopolitan Syncopaters on Simcha)			10002, May M1-2019
My Capri Serenade	Maurice Winnick aho	Lon	26 Mar 40	HMV BD-5582*
My Cradle Is The Desert	Radio Melody Boys (duet LA)	Lon	1 Dec 30	EBW 5203
My Hat's On The Side Of My Head	Ray Noble aho	Lon	27 Oct 33	HMV B-6421, Vic 24624
My Heart Is Taking Lessons	Geraldo aho	Lon	9 Sep 38	HMV BD-5402
My Heart's To Let	Ray Noble aho	Lon	27 Feb 33	HMV B-6323, Vic 24341
My Heart's To Let	Lew Stone and the Mons Band	Lon	2 Mar 33	Dec F-3496
My Heaven On Earth	Maurice Winnick and his Sweet Music	Lon	13 Jun 38	Dec F-6696*
My Melancholy Baby	AB acc orc dir Ray Noble	NY	15 Mar 35	HMV B-8330, BD-228, Vic 25007
My Melancholy Baby	AB acc Monia Liter (p)	Lon	–– Aug 36	WR SH370+, EMI GX 2512+ FS
My Own	Geraldo aho	Lon	16 Dec 38	HMV BD-5444*
My Regular Girl	AB acc Heinz Lewy (p)	Ber	18 Nov 27	Hom 4-2416
My Regular Girl	Arthur Briggs' Sav Syn Orc	Ber	–– Oct 27	DG/Pol 21131
My Regular Girl	John Abriani's Six	Ber	18 Jan 28	Hom 4-2512,
My Romance	AB	Lon	7 Oct 32	Dec F-3218
My Song Goes Round The World	Ray Noble aho	Lon	7 Dec 33	HMV B-6438, Vic 24555
My Sunny Monterey	Buddy Lewis aho (as Jack Holmes aho on Mayfair)	Lon	1 Jun 32	Pan 25240, May G-2170
My Sunshine Came On A Rainy Day	Radio Melody Boys (duet LA)	Lon	30 Dec 30	EBR 1447
My Sweet	Ray Noble aho	Lon	27 Apr 34	HMV B-6484, Vic 25232

155

Title	Artiste	Place	Date	Original Issue
My Sweetie Went Away	New Mayfair Orc	Lon	14 Jul 31	HMV B-4012
My Sweet Virginia	Roy Fox ahb	Lon	7 Mar 32	Dec F-2866
My Sweet Virginia	Durium Dance Band	Lon	1 Apr 32	Durium EN-9
My Temptation	Roy Fox ahb	Lon	5 May 31	Dec F-2329
My Woman	Lew Stone and the Mons Band	Lon	29 Nov 32	Dec F-3313*
'Neath Hawaiian Skies	Palm Beach Hawaiians	Lon	9 Feb 31	Dec F-2255
'Neath The Spell of Monte Carlo	Roy Fox ahb	Lon	5 Nov 31	Dec F-2683
Never Break A Promise	Geraldo aho	Lon	11 Nov 38	HMV BD-5428*
Never Swat A Fly	Marius B. Winter and his Dance Orc	Lon	–– Dec 30	Bdcst 2606
Never Swat A Fly	Blue Jays (duet LA)	Lon	9 Jan 31	EBR 1456
Nice Work If You Can Get It	Lew Stone ahb (with The Jackdaws)	Lon	2 Feb 38	AC
Nicky The Greek (Has Gone)	Al Bowlly and Jimmy Mesene acc Pat Dodd (p)	Lon	2 Apr 41	HMV BD-922
Nigger Blues	AB (with Ella Logan)	Lon	24 Nov 30	Dec F-2560
Night And Day	AB acc orc dir Carroll Gibbons	Lon	16 Oct 33	Dec F-3695
Nightfall	Lew Stone and the Mons Dance Orc	Lon	21 Oct 32	Dec rejected
Nightfall	Lew Stone and the Mons Dance Orc	Lon	31 Oct 32	Dec F-3234*
Night On The Desert	Ray Noble aho	Lon	31 May 34	HMV B-6496
Night On The Desert	Lew Stone aho	Lon	15 Jun 34	Dec F-5017*
Night On The Desert	Ray Noble aho	NY	–– –– 35	Air Aircheck 2+ RT
Night When Love Was Born, The	Roy Fox ahb	Lon	9 Sep 32	Dec F-3152
Night You Gave Me Back The Ring, The	Masqueraders (with Carlyle Cousins)	Lon	18 Feb 32	Col CB-429
Nobody Cares If I'm Blue	Waikiki Serenaders (duet LA)	Lon	–– Jan 31	Bdcst 673
Nobody's Sweetheart	Roy Fox ahb	Lon	2 Dec 31	Dec F-2716
Not Bad	Ray Noble aho	Lon	12 Mar 34	HMV B-6471, Vic 24619
Now	Ray Noble aho	NY	16 Oct 36	HMV BD-5287*, Vic 25448*
Now	Ray Noble aho	NY	7 Dec 36	Lon HMG-5019+ RT

Title	Artiste	Place	Date	Original Issue
Now It Can Be Told	Lew Stone ahb	Lon	27 Sep 38	Dec F-6795*
Now That You're Gone	Durium Dance Band	Lon	1 Apr 32	Durium EN-11
Oceans Of Time	Ray Noble aho	Lon	7 Dec 33	HMV B-6450, Vic 24603
Oh! Donna Clara	Waikiki Serenaders (duet LA)	Lon	-- Jan 31	Bdcst 673
Oh! Donna Clara	Palm Beach Hawaiians (duet LA)	Lon	23 Jan 31	Dec F-2213
Oh! Johanna	NMDO	Lon	19 Sep 33	HMV B-6397
Oh! Mr Moon	Scott-Wood Accordion Quartet	Lon	3 Apr 33	Parl R-1476
Oh! Mr Moon	Lew Stone and the Mons Band	Lon	5 Apr 33	Dec F-3535
Oh! Mr Moon	Lew Stone ahb	Lon	13 Jun 33	AC
Oh! Rosalita	Jack Leon ahb	Lon	-- Jun 31	Pic 788
Okay, Baby	Blue Jays (duet LA)	Lon	30 Dec 30	EBR 1448
Okay, Baby	Marius B. Winter and his Dance Orc (with unknown)	Lon	-- Jan 31	Bdcst 3004
Old Covered Bridge, The	Ray Noble aho	Lon	21 Apr 34	HMV B-6484
Old Fashioned Girl – see 'There's Something About An Old Fashioned Girl'				
Old Italian Love Song, An	Linn Milford and his Haw Sing	Lon	24 Jan 30	Reg MR-28
Old Man Of The Mountain, The	Roy Fox ahb	Lon	23 Sep 32	Dec F-3181
Old New England Moon	Waikiki Serenaders (duet LA)	Lon	-- Nov 30	Bdcst 644
Old Spanish Moon	Hawaiian Serenaders	Lon	13 Nov 30	Victory 302
Old Spinning Wheel, The	Ray Noble aho	Lon	10 May 33	HMV B-6348
On A Little Balcony In Spain	New Mayfair Orc	Lon	29 May 31	HMV B-3881
On A Little Dream Ranch	AB	Lon	19 Jun 37	HMV BD-434
On A Steamer Coming Over	Ray Noble aho	Lon	20 Dec 33	HMV B-6440
Once In A While	Maurice Winnick and his Sweet Music	Lon	20 Jan 38	Dec F-6599*
One Day When We Were Young	Geraldo aho	Lon	10 Jan 39	HMV BD-5449*

Title	Artiste	Place	Date	Original Issue
One Day When We Were Young	Geraldo aho	Lon	– – – – 39	Hal Hal-14 + RT
One Hour With You	New Mayfair Orc	Lon	3 May 32	HMV B-4188
One Little Quarrel	Ray Noble and his NMDO	Lon	19 Dec 31	HMV B-6118
One Little Quarrel	Masqueraders (with Anona Winn)	Lon	14 Jan 32	Col CB-413
One More Affair	Roy Fox ahb	Lon	20 Jul 32	Dec F-3093
One More Kiss	Durium Dance Band	Lon	15 Mar 32	Durium EN-0
One More Time	Roy Fox ahb	Lon	25 Mar 31	Dec F-2294
One Morning In May	Ray Noble aho	Lon	5 Apr 34	HMV B-6478
One Night Alone With You	Al Vocale and his Crooners (duet LA)	Lon	– – Sep 30	EBR 1389
One, Two, Button Your Shoe	Ray Noble aho	NY	25 Sep 36	Vic 25428*
Only Forever	Al Bowlly and Jimmy Mesene	Lon	6 Dec 40	HMV BD-892
Only Me Knows Why	Masqueraders	Lon	18 Feb 32	Col CB-428
On The Other Side Of Lover's Lane	Ray Noble aho	Lon	13 Jul 33	HMV B-6380, Vic 24420
On The Sentimental Side	Geraldo aho	Lon	9 Sep 38	HMV BD-5402
On The Sentimental Side	Lew Stone ahb	Lon	27 Sep 38	Dec F-6795*
On The Sunny Side Of The Street	Aldwych Players dir Jay Wilbur	Lon	2 Aug 30	Victory 253
Ooh! That Kiss	Roy Fox ahb	Lon	8 Aug 32	Dec F-3099
Ou Kaapstad Is Mij Hemel-Land (in Afrikaans)	AB acc Gideon Fagan (p)	Hay	10 Jun 30	HMV rejected
Ou Kaapstad Is Mij Hemel-Land (in Afrikaans)	AB	Hay	14 Jul 30	HMV FJ-100
Ou Lelie Valley, Die (in Afrikaans)	AB	Hay	10 Oct 30	HMV FJ-120
Out Of Nowhere	Roy Fox ahb	Lon	31 Jul 31	Dec F-2439*
Outside Of Paradise	Al Bowlly aho	NY	3 Dec 37	BB B-7319*
Over My Shoulder	Ray Noble aho	Lon	2 Jul 34	HMV B-6504, Vic 24720
Overnight	Roy Fox ahb	Lon	26 Feb 31	Dec F-2256
Over On The Sunny Side	Ray Noble aho	Lon	21 Feb 34	HMV B-6463
Over The Blue	Roy Fox ahb	Lon	5 Nov 31	Dec F-2683
Over The Blue	Howard Godfrey and his Waldorfians	Lon	– – Nov 31	Pic 856

Title	Artiste	Place	Date	Original Issue
Over The Rainbow	AB acc orc dir Ronnie Munro	Lon	21 Dec 39	HMV BD-808
Pagan Love Song, The	Honolulu Serenaders (duet LA)	Lon	–– Nov 29	Dom A-219
Pagan Moon	Ray Noble and the NMDO	Lon	20 Jul 32	HMV B-6219
Pagan Serenade	NMDO	Lon	14 Aug 31	HMV B-6055
Pale Volga Moon	Scott-Wood Accordion Quartet	Lon	3 Apr 33	Parl R-1469
Pardon Me, Pretty Baby	Maurice Winnick aho	Lon	10 Jul 31	Reg MR-374
Paris In The Spring	Ray Noble aho	NY	10 May 35	HMV BD-192*, Vic 25040*
Peach Of A Pair, A	Roy Fox ahb	Lon	28 Jan 31	Dec F-2233
Peanut Vendor, The	Roy Fox ahb	Lon	9 Feb 31	Dec F-2239
Pennies From Heaven	Monia Liter and the Ace of Hearts Orc	Lon	–– –– 38	Sav Svl-168+ RT
Penny Serenade	Geraldo aho	Lon	11 Nov 38	HMV BD-5428*
Penny Serenade	Lew Stone ahb	Lon	28 Nov 38	Dec F-6890*
Penny Serenade	Geraldo aho	Lon	–– –– 39	Hal Hal-13+ RT
Pettin' In The Park	Ray Noble aho	Lon	5 Jul 33	HMV B-6375
Piccolino, The	Ray Noble aho	NY	9 Apr 35	RT
Piccolino, The	Ray Noble aho	NY	10 Jun 35	HMV BD-247*, Vic 25094*
Pied Piper of Hamelin	Ray Noble and the NMDO	Lon	4 Dec 31	HMV B-6112, Vic 24034
Play, Fiddle, Play	NMDO	Lon	31 Jan 33	HMV B-6318
Please	Ray Noble aho	Lon	8 Dec 32	HMV B-6283
Please Don't Mention It	Ray Noble and the NMDO (with Anona Winn)	Lon	20 Jul 32	HMV B-6219
Please Don't Mention It	AB	Lon	26 Jul 32	Dec F-3128, M-422
Please Handle With Care	Lew Stone and the Mons Band	Lon	27 Jan 33	Dec F-3456
Please Keep Me In Your Dreams	Ray Noble aho	NY	–– –– 36	RT
Poor Kid	Roy Fox ahb	Lon	16 Jun 31	Dec F-2396*
Poor Kid	Blue Jays	Lon	–– Aug 31	EBR 1541
Poor Me, Poor You	NMDO	Lon	7 Jan 33	HMV B-6318

159

Title	Artiste	Place	Date	Original Issue
Positively, Absolutely	AB acc Heinz Lewy (p)	Ber	18 Nov 27	Hom 4-2461
Pretty Kitty Kelly	New Mayfair Orc	Lon	29 May 31	HMV B-3881
Pretty Little Patchwork Quilt, The	AB acc orc dir Ronnie Munro	Lon	2 Feb 38	HMV BD-503
Prisoner Of Love	Roy Fox ahb	Lon	7 Jan 32	Dec rejected
Prisoner Of Love	Roy Fox ahb	Lon	21 Jan 32	Dec F-2775
Prisoner's Song, The – see 'Banditlied'				
Prize Waltz, The	Ray Noble aho	Lon	24 Aug 34	HMV B-6516
Proud Of You	Oscar Rabin and his Romany Band	Lon	28 Sep 38	Rex 9384*
Put That Sun Back In The Sky	Roy Fox ahb	Lon	19 May 32	Dec F-3015
Put Your Little Arms Around Me	Ray Noble and the NMDO	Lon	8 Jan 32	HMV B-6131
Rain (unconfirmed)	Billy Bartholomew's Delphians	Ber	– – Jun 28	DG/Pol 21663
Rain On The Roof	Durium Dance Band	Lon	20 Apr 32	Durium EN-12
Rain, Rain, Go Away	Lew Stone and the Mons Dance Orc	Lon	21 Oct 32	Dec rejected
Rain, Rain, Go Away	Lew Stone and the Mons Dance Orc	Lon	31 Oct 32	Dec F-3233*
Reaching For The Moon	Roy Fox ahb	Lon	5 Mar 31	Dec F-2279
Reaching For The Moon	New Mayfair Orc	Lon	26 Jun 31	HMV B-3910
Really Mine	Palm Beach Hawaiians	Lon	9 Feb 31	Dec F-2246
Really Mine	NMDO	Lon	19 Feb 31	HMV B-5989
Really Mine	Percy Chandler ahb	Lon	– – Apr 31	Pic 764, Oct 608
Red Maple Leaves, The	Lew Stone ahb	Lon	15 Aug 38	Dec F-6777*
Red Sails In The Sunset	AB acc orc dir Ray Noble	NY	18 Sep 35	HMV BD-295, Vic 25142
Remember Me	Ray Noble aho	Lon	6 Jul 34	HMV B-6508
Ridin' Home	AB acc orc dir Ronnie Munro	Lon	5 Oct 39	HMV BD-776
Riding On A Haycart Home	Lew Stone ahb	Lon	3 May 34	Dec F-5004
Rio De Janeiro	Deauville Dance Band	Lon	– – Nov 31	EBR 1584
Rio Rita	Fred Bird, The Salon Symphonic Jazz Band	Ber	– – Dec 27	Hom 4-2496

Title	Artiste	Place	Date	Original Issue
Rio Rita (unconfirmed)	Jay Wilbur and his Band (duet Cavan O'Connor)	Lon	— Feb 30	Dom A-246
Riptide	Lew Stone ahb	Lon	15 Jun 34	Dec F-5017*
River, Stay 'Way From My Door	New Mayfair Orc	Lon	26 Jun 31	HMV B-3910
Roamin' Thru' The Roses	Marius B. Winter and his Dance Orc	Lon	— Dec 30	Bdcst 2607
Rock Your Cares Away	Ray Noble and the NMDO	Lon	11 Oct 32	HMV B-6250, Vic 24302, Vic 25262
Roll Along, Prairie Moon	AB acc orc dir Ray Noble	NY	18 Sep 35	HMV BD-295, Vic 25142
Rolling Home	Lew Stone ahb	Lon	1 Aug 34	Dec F-5172
Roll On, Mississippi, Roll On	NMDO (with Three Ginx)	Lon	11 Jun 31	HMV B-6040
Roll On, Mississippi, Roll On	Roy Fox ahb	Lon	31 Jul 31	Dec F-2438
Roll On, Mississippi, Roll On	Sid Phillips and his Melodians	Lon	— Aug 31	EBW 5358
Roll On, Mississippi, Roll On	Deauville Dance Band	Lon	— Sep 31	EBR 1550
Roll Up The Carpet	Ray Noble aho	Lon	12 Jul 33	HMV B-6380, Vic 24420, 25262
Romany	AB acc orc dir Ronnie Munro	Lon	14 Feb 39	HMV BD-666
Romany	Geraldo aho	Lon	— — — 39	Hal Hal-14 + RT
Rosalie	New Mayfair Orc dir Ronnie Munro	Lon	14 Jan 38	HMV BD-502*
Rosalie	Maurice Winnick and his Sweet Music	Lon	20 Jan 38	Dec F-6605*
Rosa Mia	AB acc orc dir George Scott-Wood	Lon	15 Nov 32	Dec F-3275
Rose Dreams	Linn Milford and his Haw Pla	Lon	19 Sep 30	Reg MR-216
Roses For Remembrance	Arthur Briggs' Sav Syn Orc	Ber	— Oct 27	DG/Pol 21128
Rosy Cheeks	AB acc Heinz Lewy (p)	Ber	18 Nov 27	Hom 4-2460
Rosy Cheeks	Arthur Briggs' Sav Syn Orc	Ber	— Oct 27	DG/Pol 21127
Roy Fox's Commentary On Minnie The Moocher's Wedding	Roy Fox ahb	Lon	20 Jul 32	Dec F-3063

Title	Artiste	Place	Date	Original Issue
Sailing On The Robert E. Lee	Masqueraders	Lon	24 Mar 32	Col CB-443
Sailing On The Robert E. Lee	Ray Noble and the NMDO	Lon	3 May 32	HMV B-6176, Vic 24128
St Louis Blues	Ray Noble aho	NY	10 Jun 35	HMV BD-5004*, Vic 25082*
Sal Die Eng'le Hul Harpe Speel Vir Mij? (in Afrikaans)	AB	Hay	10 Oct 30	HMV FJ-103
Same Old Story, The	Geraldo aho	Lon	7 Mar 39	HMV BD-5467*
Save The Last Dance For Me	Savoy Hotel Orpheans	Lon	16 Feb 32	Col CB-426
Save The Last Dance For Me	Durium Dance Band	Lon	15 Mar 32	Durium EN-8
Say A Little Prayer For Me	Al Vocale and his Crooners (duet LA)	Lon	–– Sep 30	EBR 1416
Say Goodnight To Your Old-fashioned Mother	Lew Stone ahb	Lon	15 Aug 38	Dec F-6763*
Say It With A Red, Red Rose	John Abriani's Six	Ber	18 Jan 28	Hom 4-2524
Say, Mister! Have You Met Rosie's Sister	AB acc Edgar Adeler (p)	Ber	18 Aug 27	Hom 4-2386
Say To Yourself 'I Will Be Happy'	Lew Stone ahb	Lon	–––– 33	FS
Say When	Victor Young aho	NY	2 Nov 34	Dec 278*
Seven Years With The Wrong Woman	Ray Noble aho	Lon	24 May 33	HMV B-6364, Vic 24388
Shadow Waltz, The	Ray Noble aho	Lon	5 Jul 33	HMV B-6376
Shady Tree, A	John Abriani's Six	Ber	18 Jan 28	Hom 4-2511*
Shake And Let Us Be Friends	Jack Leon ahb	Lon	–– Jun 31	Pic 802
Shakin' The Blues Away	John Abriani's Six	Ber	18 Jan 28	Hom 4-2514
She Didn't Say 'Yes'	Masqueraders	Lon	11 Mar 32	Col DB-782
She Didn't Say 'Yes'	Roy Fox ahb (as part of a trio)	Lon	22 Mar 32	Dec F-2888
She Loves Me Not	Ray Noble aho	Lon	27 Apr 34	HMV B-6485
She's My Secret Passion	Phantom Players dir Len Fillis	Lon	3 Nov 30	Dec F-2144
She's My Secret Passion (on label as 'He's My . . .')	Earl Melville and his Hawaiians	Lon	–– Nov 30	Pic 649

Title	Artiste	Place	Date	Original Issue
She Was Poor But She Was Honest – see 'Sy Was Arm Maar Sy Was Eirlik'				
Shoe Shine Boy	Monia Liter and the Ace of Hearts Orc	Lon	– – – – 38	Sav Svl-168+ RT
Shout For Happiness	NMDO	Lon	19 Feb 31	HMV B-5984
Shout For Happiness	Roy Fox ahb	Lon	26 Feb 31	Dec F-2263
Show Is Over, The	Ray Noble aho	Lon	31 May 34	HMV B-6492
Side By Side (unconfirmed)	Billy Bartholomew's Delphians	Ber	– – May 28	DG/Pol 21605
Silver Toned Chimes Of The Angelus, The	Linn Milford and his Haw Pla	Lon	17 Dec 30	Reg MR-267
Silv'ry Moon	Linn Milford and his Haw Pla	Lon	7 Mar 30	Reg MR-79
Silv'ry Moon	Honolulu Serenaders (as Hawaiian Octet on Cel)	Lon	– – Mar 30	Dom C-319, Cel 4390
Silv'ry Moon	Edgar Adeler's Hawaiian Pla	Lon	– – Mar 30	Sterno 406, Solex 6
Since I Found You	Arthur Briggs' Sav Syn Orc	Ber	– – Oct 27	DG/Pol 21125
Sing Another Chorus, Please	Roy Fox ahb	Lon	18 Sep 31	Dec F-2514
Sing As We Go	Ray Noble aho	Lon	30 Aug 34	HMV B-6514
Sing Hallelujah	Billy Bartholomew's Delphians	Ber	– – May 28	DG/Pol 21604
Si Petite	Ray Noble aho	Lon	13 Jul 33	HMV B-6381
Sittin' In The Dark	Jack Jackson aho	Lon	24 Feb 33	HMV B-6322
Sleepy Head	Al Vocale and his Crooners (duet LA)	Lon	24 Oct 30	EBW 5189
Sleepy Head	Edgar Adeler's Haw Pla	Lon	– – Nov 30	Sterno 594
Sleepy Head	Linn Milford and his Haw Pla	Lon	17 Dec 30	Reg MR-337
Small Fry	Geraldo aho	Lon	14 Oct 38	HMV BD-5421*
Small Town	Reginald Williams and his Futurists	Lon	5 May 39	Col FB-2226
Smile, Darn You, Smile	Roy Fox ahb	Lon	7 Oct 31	Dec F-2580
Smile When You Say Goodbye	Ronnie Munro aho	Lon	17 Jul 37	HMV BD-5248
Snowball	Ray Noble aho	Lon	21 Oct 33	HMV B-6408
Snowball	Ray Noble aho	NY	13 May 35	Lon HMG-5027+RT

Title	Artiste	Place	Date	Original Issue
Snuggled On Your Shoulder	Savoy Hotel Orpheans	Lon	11 May 32	Col CB-458
So Ashamed	AB acc orc dir George Scott-Wood	Lon	15 Nov 32	Dec F-3275
Solitude	Ray Noble aho	NY	17 Apr 35	JA JA-22+ RT
Somebody Loves You	Roy Fox ahb	Lon	13 Apr 32	Dec F-2922
Somebody Ought To Be Told	Ray Noble aho	NY	9 Dec 35	Vic 25200*
Somebody's Thinking Of You Tonight	Maurice Winnick and his Sweet Music	Lon	13 Jun 38	Dec F-6695*
Somehow	Edgar Adeler's Haw Pla	Lon	‑‑ Mar 30	Sterno 429
Someone To Care For	Lew Stone and the Mons Band	Lon	2 Mar 33	Dec F-3502
Something Came And Got Me In The Spring	NMDO	Lon	16 Jun 33	HMV B-6369
Something To Sing About	Mantovani aho	Lon	4 Mar 38	Col FB-1925
Sometimes	Van Phillips ahb	Lon	12 Nov 28	Col 5209
Sometimes I'm Happy	Arthur Briggs' Sav Syn Orc	Ber	‑‑ Oct 27	DG/Pol 21127
Somewhere In France With You	AB acc orc dir Ronnie Munro	Lon	21 Dec 39	HMV BD-805
Somewhere In Old Wyoming	Ferrachini's Haw Band (duet LA)	Lon	‑‑ Jan 31	Bdcst 3008
Somewhere In Old Wyoming	Palm Beach Hawaiians (duet LA)	Lon	23 Jan 31	Dec F-2213
Song Of Happiness	Roy Fox ahb	Lon	2 Oct 31	Dec F-2574
Song Of The Bells	Ray Noble and the NMDO	Lon	11 Oct 32	HMV B-6249
Song of The Dawn	Aldwych Players dir Jay Wilbur (with Hubert Wallace)	Lon	2 Aug 30	Victory 252
Song Of The Wanderer	Arthur Briggs' Sav Syn Orc	Ber	‑‑ Oct 27	DG/Pol 21034
Song Without Words	Ray Noble aho	Lon	29 Nov 33	HMV B-6438, Vic 24555
Song Without Words	Ray Noble aho	NY	24 Apr 35	JA JA-22+ RT
Soon	Ray Noble aho	NY	9 Feb 35	HMV BD-140*, Vic 24879*
Soon	Ray Noble aho	NY	‑‑‑‑ 35	RT
Sorry (unconfirmed)	Billy Bartholomew's Delphians	Ber	‑‑ May 28	DG/Pol 21607

164

Title	Artiste	Place	Date	Original Issue
South Of The Border	AB acc orc dir Ronnie Munro	Lon	11 May 39	HMV BD-706
Souvenir Of Love	Sidney Lipton and his Grosvenor House Orc	Lon	13 Jan 38	Dec F-6653*
Souvenirs	Arthur Briggs' Sav Syn Orc	Ber	-- Oct 27	DG/Pol 21122
Souvenirs	Fred Bird, The Salon Symphonic Jazz Band	Ber	-- Dec 27	Hom 4-2496
S'posing	Honolulu Serenaders (duet LA)	Lon	-- Nov 29	Dom A-242
Springtime Reminds Me Of You	Maurice Winnick aho	Lon	10 Jul 31	Reg MR-375
Standing On The Corner	Ray Noble aho	Lon	7 Feb 33	HMV B-6317, Vic 24308
Star Dust	Don Barrigo and his Haw Swing	Lon	22 Aug 38	Parl rejected
Stay On The Right Side Of The Road	Ray Noble aho	Lon	16 Mar 33	HMV B-6331, Vic 24375
Stormy Weather	AB acc George Scott-Wood (pipe organ)	Lon	25 May 38	HMV rejected
Straight From The Shoulder	Lew Stone ahb	Lon	3 Aug 34	Dec F-5158
Summer's End	Geraldo aho	Lon	16 Dec 38	HMV BD-5443*
Sunny Days	Marius B. Winter and his Dance Orc with unknown	Lon	-- Dec 30	Bdcst 2607
Sunny Days	NMDO	Lon	31 Dec 30	HMV B-5956
Sunny Disposish	George Carhart's New Yorkers Jazz Orc	Ber	28 Sep 27	Hom 4-2420
Sunshine	AB acc Albert Diggenhof (p)	Hay	30 Jun 30	HMV rejected
Sunshine	AB	Hay	14 Jul 30	HMV FJ-133
Sunshine And Shadows	NMDO	Lon	26 Mar 31	HMV B-6010
Swanee	New Mayfair Orc	Lon	14 Jul 31	HMV B-3944
Sweeping The Clouds Away	Aldwych Players dir Jay Wilbur	Lon	2 Aug 30	Victory 254
Sweet And Lovely	Roy Fox ahb	Lon	18 Sep 31	Dec F-2514
Sweet And Lovely	Savoy Hotel Orpheans	Lon	19 Oct 31	Col rejected
Sweet And Lovely	Savoy Hotel Orpheans	Lon	29 Oct 31	Col CB-376
Sweet As A Song	Al Bowlly aho	NY	3 Dec 37	BB B-7317*
Sweet As A Song	AB with his Crooners Choir (The Five Herons) acc Violet Carson (p)	Lon	1 Apr 38	HMV BD-543

Title	Artiste	Place	Date	Original Issue
Sweet Genevieve	Lew Stone ahb	Lon	21 Mar 38	Dec F-6642*
Sweetheart	NMDO	Lon	20 Feb 33	HMV B-6320
Sweetheart	Ray Noble aho	Lon	17 Mar 33	HMV test
Sweetheart	Scott-Wood Accordion Quartet	Lon	3 Apr 33	Parl R-1476
Sweetheart Darlin'	Ray Noble aho	Lon	2 Jul 34	HMV rejected
Sweetheart In My Dreams Tonight	Ray Noble and the NMDO	Lon	12 Feb 32	HMV B-6146, Vic 24173
Sweetheart In My Dreams Tonight	Savoy Hotel Orpheans	Lon	16 Feb 32	Col CB-425
Sweetheart Lane – see 'Minnarslaan'				
Sweetheart Of Sigma Chi (unconfirmed)	Billy Bartholomew's Delphians	Ber	–– May 28	DG/Pol 21595
Sweet Is The Word For You	AB	Lon	5 Jul 37	HMV BD-440
Sweet Jennie Lee	Harry Hudson's Melody Men (duet LA)	Lon	9 Jan 31	EBR 1458
Sweet Jennie Lee	Blue Jays (duet LA)	Lon	3 Mar 31	EBW 5242
Sweet Marie	Arthur Briggs' Sav Syn Orc	Ber	–– Oct 27	DG/Pol 21134
Sweet Someone	AB with his Crooners Choir (The Five Herons) acc Violet Carson (p)	Lon	1 Apr 38	HMV BD-543
Sweet Stranger	Al Bowlly aho	NY	3 Dec 37	BB B-7332*
Sy's In Die Pad (in Afrikaans)	AB acc Gideon Fagan (p)	Hay	10 Jun 30	HMV FJ-133
Sy's Mij Klein Liefie (in Afrikaans)	AB acc Albert Diggenhof (p)	Hay	30 Jun 30	HMV rejected
Sy Was Arm Maar Sy Was Eirlik (in Afrikaans)	AB as Jannie Viljoen acc Claude Ivy (p)	Lon	30 Oct 30	Dec rejected
Take Away The Moon	Masqueraders	Lon	5 Mar 32	Col CB-435
Take It From Me	Roy Fox ahb	Lon	7 Oct 31	Dec F-2582
Take Your Finger Out Of Your Mouth	Arthur Briggs' Sav Syn Orc	Ber	–– Oct 27	DG/Pol 21134
Tango Lady	Percy Chandler ahb (as Alberta Dance Orc on Empire, as Argentine Tango Orc on May)	Lon	–– Apr 31	Pic 764, Empire E-7, May G-2031, Oct 608
Tap Your Feet	Radio Rhythm Boys	Lon	–– Feb 31	EBR 1489

Title	Artiste	Place	Date	Original Issue
Tell Me, Are You From Georgia?	Roy Fox ahb (with Nat Gonella)	Lon	18 Aug 31	Dec F-2451*
Tell Me You Love Me	Sid Phillips and his Melodians	Lon	–– Aug 31	EBW 5356
Tell Tales	Masqueraders	Lon	5 Mar 32	Col CB-435
Thanks	Lew Stone ahb	Lon	24 Oct 33	Dec F-3722
Thanks	Ray Noble aho	Lon	27 Oct 33	HMV B-6413
Thanks For Everything	Geraldo aho	Lon	4 Apr 39	HMV BD-5472
Thank You Most Sincerely	Waldorfians dir Howard Godfrey (as Cosmopolitan Syncopators on Simcha)	Lon	–– Jun 31	Pic 781, Oct 613, Simcha 10002
Thank Your Father	Roy Fox ahb	Lon	5 Jan 31	Dec F-2312
That Lindy Hop	Roy Fox ahb	Lon	10 Mar 31	Dec F-2250
That Little Lock Of Hair	Linn Milford and his Haw Pla	Lon	19 Sep 30	Reg MR-216
That Little Lock Of Hair	Earl Melville and his Hawaiians (with unknown)	Lon	–– Nov 30	Pic 673
That's All That Matters To Me	AB	Lon	20 Apr 33	Dec F-3560
That's Me Without You	AB	Lon	4 Jan 34	Dec F-3853
That's My Song Of Love	Al Vocale and his Crooners (duet LA)	Lon	24 Oct 30	EBW 5189
That's My Song Of Love	Earl Melville and his Hawaiians (with unknown)	Lon	–– Nov 30	Pic 673
That's Somerset	NMDO	Lon	28 Apr 31	HMV B-6011
That's What I Like About You	Roy Fox ahb	Lon	7 Oct 31	Dec F-2581
That's What I Like About You	Howard Godfrey and his Waldorfians	Lon	–– Nov 31	Pic 849
That's What Life Is Made Of	Ray Noble aho	Lon	10 May 33	HMV B-6361, Vic 24599
That's What Loneliness Means To Me	Palm Beach Hawaiians	Lon	18 Dec 30	Dec F-2246
Them There Eyes	Roy Fox ahb (with chorus)	Lon	10 Mar 31	Dec F-2252
There's A Boy Coming Home On Leave	Maurice Winnick aho	Lon	26 Mar 40	HMV BD-5583*
There's A Cabin In The Pines	Ray Noble aho	Lon	13 Jul 33	HMV B-6379

Title	Artiste	Place	Date	Original Issue
There's A Cabin In The Pines	AB	Lon	26 Jul 33	Dec F-3638
There's A Gold Mine In The Sky	Maurice Winnick and his Sweet Music	Lon	29 Dec 37	Dec F-6590*
There's A Ring Around The Moon	Ray Noble and the NMDO	Lon	3 Mar 32	HMV B-6154, Vic 24149
There's A Stranger In Heaven Tonight	Hawaiian Quartet	Lon	24 Sep 30	Dec F-1991
There's A Stranger In Heaven Tonight	Earl Melville and his Hawaiians	Lon	–– Nov 30	Pic 685
There's A Stranger In Heaven Tonight	Linn Milford and his Haw Pla	Lon	17 Dec 30	Reg MR-267
There's A Time And Place For Everything	Savoy Hotel Orpheans	Lon	19 Oct 31	Col CB-376
There's A Time And Place For Everything	Savoy Hotel Orpheans	Lon	29 Oct 31	Col rejected
There's Rain In My Eyes	AB	Lon	11 Nov 38	Dec F-6877
There's Something About An Old-fashioned Girl	Blue Jays (duet LA)	Lon	9 Jan 31	EBR 1456
There's Something About An Old-fashioned Girl	Marius B. Winter and his Dance Orc	Lon	–– Jan 31	Bdcst 3003
There's Something In The Air	Ray Noble aho	NY	16 Oct 36	HMV BD-5153*, Vic 25459*
There's Something In The Air	Ray Noble aho	NY	7 Dec 36	Lon HMG-5019+ RT
There's Something In Your Eyes	NMDO	Lon	14 Aug 31	HMV B-6056
There's Something In Your Eyes	Roy Fox ahb	Lon	30 Dec 31	Dec rejected
There's Something In Your Eyes	Roy Fox ahb	Lon	7 Jan 32	Dec F-2760
They Say	Geraldo aho	Lon	10 Jan 39	HMV BD-5448*
This Is Heaven	Honolulu Serenaders (duet LA)	Lon	–– Nov 29	Dom A-242
This Is My Love Song	Arthur Lally aho (as Jack Holmes aho on Mayfair)	Lon	21 Sep 32	Pan 25303, May G-2203
This Is Romance	Ray Noble aho	Lon	9 Nov 33	HMV B-6422
This Is The Day Of Days	NMDO	Lon	31 Oct 31	HMV B-6091

Title	Artiste	Place	Date	Original Issue
This Is The Missus	Roy Fox ahb	Lon	5 Nov 31	Dec F-2682
This Little Piggie Went To Market	Ray Noble aho	Lon	16 Feb 34	HMV B-6461
This Year's Roses	Macari aho	Lon	4 May 40	Reg rejected
Three Wishes	Ray Noble aho	Lon	16 Mar 33	HMV B-6332, Vic 24347
Three Wishes	Lew Stone and the Mons Band	Lon	5 Apr 33	Dec F-3534
Tid-dle-id-dle-um-pum	Blue Jays (duet LA)	Lon	3 Mar 31	EBW 5242
Tie A Little String Around Your Finger	Roy Fox ahb	Lon	21 Jul 31	Dec F-2403*
Time Alone Will Tell	Sid Phillips and his Melodians	Lon	–– Aug 31	EBW 5356
Time Alone Will Tell	Roy Fox ahb	Lon	18 Sep 31	Dec F-2513
Time On My Hands	NMDO	Lon	19 Feb 31	HMV B-5983, Vic 25016
Time On My Hands	Roy Fox ahb	Lon	25 Mar 31	Dec F-2291
Time On My Hands	Waldorfians dir Howard Godfrey (as Basil Winston aho on Empire, as Percy Chandler aho on May)	Lon	–– Jun 31	Pic 787, Oct 617, Empire E-9, May G-2017
Time On My Hands	Deauville Dance Band	Lon	–– Jun 31	EBW 5315
Ti-pi-tin	Lew Stone ahb	Lon	21 Apr 38	Dec F-6664*
To Be Worthy Of You	Roy Fox ahb	Lon	21 Jan 32	Dec F-2793
To Mother, With Love	Geraldo aho	Lon	4 Apr 39	HMV BD-5473
Top Hat	Ray Noble aho (with Ray Noble and the Freshmen)	NY	8 Jun 35	HMV BD-247*, Vic 25094*
Torn Sails	AB acc Claude Bampton (p)	Lon	–– –– 39	Pres Joy D281 + PR
Touch Of Your Lips, The	Ray Noble aho	NY	19 Mar 36	Vic 25277*
Touch Of Your Lips, The	Ray Noble and his London Orc 'Ray Noble Medley'	Lon	24 Aug 36	HMV C-2872*, Vic 36194*
Trouble In Paradise	Ray Noble aho	Lon	19 Sep 33	HMV B-6394
True	AB acc Monia Liter (p)	Lon	9 Apr 34	Dec F-3963
Truly	Roy Fox ahb (with chorus)	Lon	10 Mar 31	Dec F-2292
Trusting My Luck	Sidney Lipton and his Grosvenor House Orc	Lon	13 Jan 38	Dec F-6653*
Try To Forget	Masqueraders	Lon	11 Mar 32	Col DB-782

169

Title	Artiste	Place	Date	Original Issue
Turn On The Old Music Box	Maurice Winnick aho	Lon	1 Mar 40	HMV BD-5573
Turn Your Money In Your Pocket	Al Bowlly and Jimmy Mesene	Lon	12 Sep 40	HMV BD-865
Twentieth Century Blues	New Mayfair Novelty Orc	Lon	14 Nov 31	HMV B-4001, Vic 24090
Two Sleepy People	Geraldo aho	Lon	3 Dec 38	HMV BD-5437*
Underneath The Spanish Stars	Radio Melody Boys (duet LA)	Lon	30 Dec 30	EBR 1447
Underneath The Spanish Stars	NMDO	Lon	31 Dec 30	HMV B-5955
Under The Moon	Billy Bartholomew's Delphians (with Billy Bartholomew)	Ber	–– May 28	DG/Pol 21604
Under Your Spell	Ray Noble aho	NY	7 Dec 36	Lon HMG-5027+ RT
Unless	Ray Noble aho	Lon	1 Feb 34	HMV B-6453
Up In The Clouds	Percival Mackey and his Concert Orc (as the 'Ever Bright Boys' on Pic)	Lon	–– Apr 29	Pic 264, Met 1141, Oct 291
Vamp Till Ready	Lew Stone ahb	Lon	15 Feb 34	Dec F-3906
Very Thought Of You, The	AB acc Monia Liter (p)	Lon	9 Apr 34	Dec F-3963
Very Thought Of You, The	Ray Noble aho	Lon	21 Apr 34	HMV B-6482, Vic 24657
Very Thought Of You, The	AB acc Monia Liter (p)	Lon	–– Apr 34	FS
Vieni, Vieni	Ronnie Munro aho	Lon	17 Jul 37	HMV BD-5242*, Vic 25668*
Village Band, The	Ray Noble aho (with chorus)	Lon	25 Apr 33	HMV B-6344
Village Jazz Band, The	Billy Hill and his Boys	Lon	18 Dec 30	Dec F-2172
Violin In Vienna	AB acc orc dir Ronnie Munro	Lon	14 Feb 39	HMV BD-673
Vo-do-do-de-o Blues	Arthur Briggs' Sav Syn Orc	Ber	–– Oct 27	DG/Pol 21133
Voetslaan Op Oom Jacob Se Leer (in Afrikaans)	AB	Hay	10 Oct 30	HMV FJ-103

Title	Artiste	Place	Date	Original Issue
Wagon Wheels	Lew Stone ahb	Lon	15 Feb 34	Dec F-3905
Wagon Wheels	Ray Noble aho	Lon	21 Feb 34	HMV B-6469
Waiting At The End Of The Road	Linn Milford and his Haw Sing	Lon	24 Jan 28	Reg rejected
Waiting For That Thing Called Happiness	Al Vocale and his Crooners (duet LA)	Lon	24 Oct 30	EBR 1416
Walkin' My Baby Back Home	Jack Leon ahb (as Alberta Dance Band on Empire, as Jerome Joy ahb on Simcha)	Lon	––Jun 31	Pic 783, Empire E-12, Simcha 10001
Walkin' My Baby Back Home	Blue Jays	Lon	––Jun 31	EBR 1507
Walkin' Thru' Mockin' Bird Lane	AB acc orc dir Ronnie Munro	Lon	7 Mar 40	HMV BD-834
Waltzing In A Dream	Ray Noble aho	Lon	3 May 33	HMV B-6348
Waltz Of My Heart	Geraldo aho	Lon	4 Apr 39	HMV rejected
Waltz You Saved For Me, The	Maurice Winnick aho	Lon	10 Jul 31	Reg MR-375
Wanderer	Ray Noble aho	Lon	12 Jan 33	HMV B-6306, Vic 24297
Was That The Human Thing To Do?	Durium Dance Band	Lon	1 Apr 32	Durium EN-11
Was That The Human Thing To Do?	Arthur Lally aho	Lon	1 Jun 32	Dec F-3006
Waves Of The Ocean Are Whispering Goodnight, The	Bram Martin ahb	Lon	8 Jun 39	Rex 9590*
Way Back Home	Ray Noble aho (with the Freshmen)	NY	1 May 35	JA JA-22+ RT
Way Back Home	Ray Noble aho (with the Freshmen)	NY	13 May 35	Lon HMG-5027+ RT
Way With Every Sailor, The	Howard Godfrey and his Waldorfians	Lon	––Nov 31	Pic 856, Oct 134
Wedding Bells Are Ringing For Sally	Roy Fox ahb	Lon	24 Jan 31	Dec F-2219
Wedding Of The Slumtown Babies, The	Lew Stone ahb	Lon	––––33	FS
Weep No More, My Baby	Ray Noble aho	Lon	12 Oct 33	HMV B-6409
Weep No More, My Baby	Lew Stone ahb	Lon	1 Dec 33	Dec F-3783
We'll Be Together Again	Masqueraders	Lon	5 Mar 32	Col CB-434

Title	Artiste	Place	Date	Original Issue
We'll Go Smiling Along	Al Bowlly and Jimmy Mesene	Lon	12 Sep 40	HMV BD-865
Were You Sincere	AB	Lon	2 Sep 31	Dec F-2485
We Two	NMDO	Lon	24 Mar 31	HMV B-5999
We've Got The Moon And Sixpence	Ray Noble and the NMDO	Lon	21 Apr 32	HMV B-6203, Vic 24212
We've Got The Moon And Sixpence	Arthur Lally aho	Lon	23 Jul 32	Dec F-3066*
What A Fool I've Been	Maurice Winnick aho	Lon	10 Jul 31	Reg MR-374
What A Life!	Savoy Hotel Orpheans	Lon	18 Jul 32	Col CB-482
What A Little Moonlight Can Do	Lew Stone ahb	Lon	3 Aug 34	Dec F-5270
What A Perfect Night For Love	Marius B. Winter and his Dance Orc	Lon	– – Nov 30	Bdcst 2599
What A Perfect Night For Love	Blue Jays (duet LA)	Lon	1 Dec 30	EBW 5202
What Are You Thinking About, Baby?	Roy Fox ahb	Lon	3 Sep 31	Dec F-2486
What Do You Know About Love?	Reginald Williams and his Futurists	Lon	5 May 39	Col FB-2227
What Do You Know About Love?	AB acc orc dir Ronnie Munro	Lon	11 May 39	HMV BD-706
What Is There To Take Its Place?	Lew Stone ahb	Lon	25 Apr 34	Dec F-5003*
What Makes You So Adorable?	Savoy Hotel Orpheans	Lon	11 May 32	Col CB-469
What Makes You So Adorable?	New Mayfair Orc	Lon	27 May 32	HMV B-4208
What Makes You So Adorable?	Roy Fox ahb	Lon	10 Jun 32	Dec F-3028
What More Can I Ask?	Ray Noble aho	Lon	14 Dec 32	HMV B-6302, Vic 24314
What More Can I Ask?	Lew Stone and the Mons Band	Lon	23 Dec 32	Dec F-3373*
What More Can I Ask? (News Chronicle competition record)	Lew Stone and the Mons Band with AB	Lon	27 Jan 33	Dec F-3459*, Brun 6576
What More Can I Ask?	Lew Stone ahb	Lon	– – – – 33	FS
What Now?	Ray Noble aho	Lon	12 Mar 34	HMV B-6470, Vic 24711
What Would You Do?	New Mayfair Orc	Lon	3 May 32	HMV B-4188
Wheezy Anna	Ray Noble aho	Lon	7 Feb 33	HMV B-6316, Vic 24287

Title	Artiste	Place	Date	Original Issue
When Bill Malone Plays The Xylophone	Billy Hill and his Boys	Lon	18 Dec 30	Dec rejected
When Granny Wore Her Crinoline	Felix Mendelssohn aho	Lon	1 Jul 38	Dec F-6727*
When I Dream Of Home	Al Bowlly and Jimmy Mesene	Lon	18 Jul 40	HMV BD-857
When I'm With You	Ray Noble aho	NY	25 May 36	HMV BD-5091*, Vic 25336*
When It's Sunset On The Nile	Roy Fox ahb	Lon	15 Apr 31	Dec F-2315
When It's Sunset On The Nile	NMDO	Lon	25 Aug 31	HMV B-6057
When Love Comes Swinging Along	Victor Young aho	NY	2 Nov 34	Dec 278*
When Mother Nature Sings Her Lullaby	Geraldo aho	Lon	11 Nov 38	HMV BD-5427*
When Mother Nature Sings Her Lullaby	AB	Lon	11 Nov 38	Dec F-6877
When My Little Pomeranian Met Your Little Pekinese	Ray Noble aho (with Frances Day)	Lon	10 May 33	HMV B-6358
When That Man Is Dead And Gone	Al Bowlly and Jimmy Mesene acc Pat Dodd (p)	Lon	2 Apr 41	HMV BD-922
When The Lilac Blooms Again	Percival Mackey and his Concert Orc	Lon	–– Apr 29	Pic 288
When The Organ Played 'Oh Promise Me'	AB acc George Scott-Wood (pipe organ)	Lon	25 May 38	HMV BD-565
When The Organ Played 'Oh Promise Me'	Maurice Winnick and his Sweet Music	Lon	13 Jun 38	Dec F-6695*
When The Rest Of The Crowd Goes Home	Arthur Lally aho	Lon	1 Jun 32	Dec F-3006
When The Waltz Was Through	Roy Fox ahb	Lon	18 Sep 31	Dec F-2513
When We're Alone	Roy Fox ahb	Lon	13 Apr 32	Dec F-2922
When We're Alone	Savoy Hotel Orpheans	Lon	11 May 32	Col CB-459
When You Played The Organ And I Sang 'The Rosary'	AB acc Heinz Lewy (p)	Ber	18 Nov 27	Hom 4–2459
When Your Hair Has Turned To Silver	Roy Fox ahb	Lon	5 Mar 31	Dec F-2263
When You've Fallen In Love	Ray Noble aho	Lon	27 Feb 33	HMV B-6323, Vic 24341

Title	Artiste	Place	Date	Original Issue
When You've Fallen In Love	Lew Stone and the Mons Band	Lon	2 Mar 33	Dec F-3496
When You've Got A Little Springtime In Your Heart	Ray Noble aho	Lon	2 Jul 34	HMV B-6504, Vic 24720
When You Wear Your Sunday Blue	AB acc orc dir Ronnie Munro	Lon	7 Mar 40	HMV BD-827
When You Were The Blossom Of Buttercup Lane	Roy Fox ahb	Lon	21 Jul 31	Dec F-2403*
When You Were The Girl On The Scooter	Ray Noble aho (with unknown female vocalist)	Lon	29 Nov 33	HMV B-6432
When You Wish Upon A Star	Maurice Winnick aho	Lon	1 Mar 40	HMV BD-5573
Where Am I?	Ray Noble aho	NY	14 Nov 35	HMV BD-5072*, Vic 25187*
Where Are You (Girl Of My Dreams)?	Ray Noble and the NMDO (with Anona Winn)	Lon	20 Jul 32	HMV B-6220
Wherever You Are	Fred Elizalde and his Music	Lon	25 Jul 28	Brun 189
Wherever You Are (a different song to the one above)	AB	Lon	26 Jul 32	Dec F-3128, M-422
Wherever You Are	Roy Fox ahb	Lon	8 Aug 32	Dec F-3094
Where The Lazy River Goes By	Ray Noble aho	NY	16 Oct 36	HMV BD-5153*, Vic 25459*
While A Cigarette Was Burning	Geraldo aho	Lon	3 Dec 38	HMV BD-5437*
While A Cigarette Was Burning	Geraldo aho	Lon	– – – – 39	Hal Hal-14+ RT
While Hearts Are Singing	Roy Fox ahb	Lon	31 Jul 31	Dec F-2439*
Whispering	Night Club Kings	Lon	17 Jul 30	HMV rejected
Whispering	Jock McDermott ahb	Lon	5 Jan 32	EBW 5468
Whistling Waltz	Savoy Hotel Orpheans	Lon	16 Feb 32	Col CB-425
Who Am I?	Savoy Hotel Orpheans	Lon	31 Oct 31	Col CB-377
Who Do You Love?	Howard Godfrey and his Waldorfians, as Percy Chandler ahb on May	Lon	– – Nov 31	Pic 855, Oct 134, May G-2062
Who'll Buy An Old Gold Ring?	Lew Stone ahb	Lon	29 Dec 33	Dec F-3842

174

Title	Artiste	Place	Date	Original Issue
Who-oo? You-oo. That's Who!	Arthur Briggs' Sav Syn Orc	Ber	–– Oct 27	DG/Pol 21128
Who's Taking You Home Tonight?	Maurice Winnick aho	Lon	26 Mar 40	HMV BD-5582*
Who Walks In When I Walk Out?	Ray Noble aho	Lon	1 Feb 34	HMV B-6453, Vic 24594
Why Be So Unkind To Me?	Ray Noble and the NMDO	Lon	20 Jul 32	HMV B-6220
Why Couldn't You?	Percy Chandler ahb	Lon	–– Apr 31	Pic 789
Why Did You Turn Me Down?	Hawaiian Serenaders	Lon	13 Nov 30	Victory 300
Why Don't You?	Arthur Briggs' Sav Syn Orc	Ber	–– Oct 27	DG/Pol 21123
Why Dream?	Ray Noble aho	NY	20 Jul 35	HMV BD-210*, Vic 25104*
Why Stars Come Out At Night	Ray Noble aho	NY	20 Jul 35	HMV BD-210*, Vic 25105*
Why Waste Your Tears	Lew Stone and the Mons Dance Orc	Lon	21 Oct 32	Dec rejected
Why Waste Your Tears	Lew Stone and the Mons Dance Orc	Lon	31 Oct 32	Dec F-3233*
Wicked Mr Punch	Rudy Starita with Arthur Lally aho	Lon	29 Sep 32	Dec F-3186
Will The Angels Play Their Harps For Me? – see 'Sal Die Eng'le Hulle Harpe Speel Vir Mij?'				
With All My Heart	Ray Noble aho	NY	9 Dec 35	HMV BD-5028*, Vic 25209*
With All My Love And Kisses	Ray Noble and the NMDO	Lon	21 Apr 32	HMV B-6176, Vic 24128
With Love In My Heart	Ray Noble and the NMDO	Lon	3 Mar 32	HMV B-6157
With Love In My Heart	Masqueraders	Lon	5 Mar 32	Col CB-442
With My Eyes Wide Open, I'm Dreaming	Lew Stone ahb	Lon	1 Aug 34	Dec F-5172
With My Guitar And You	Edgar Adeler's Haw Pla (duet LA)	Lon	–– Nov 30	Sterno 604
With My Guitar And You	Waikiki Serenaders (duet LA)	Lon	–– Nov 30	Bdcst 643
Without A Song	Alfredo ahb (duet LA)	Lon	17 Oct 30	EBW 5187

Title	Artiste	Place	Date	Original Issue
Without A Song	New Mayfair Orc	Lon	24 Mar 31	HMV B-3836
Wonder Bar	Bohemians dir Walter Goehr	Lon	18 Apr 34	Col DX-583
Won't You Stay For Tea	Lew Stone and the Mons Band	Lon	2 Mar 33	Dec F-3502
Woodpecker Song, The	Al Bowlly and Jimmy Mesene	Lon	18 Jul 40	HMV BD-857
Woorhuis (in Afrikaans)	AB as Jannie Viljoen acc Claude Ivy (p)	Lon	30 Oct 30	Dec rejected
World Is So Small, The	Lew Stone and the Mons Band	Lon	27 Jan 33	Dec F-3455
Would You Like To Take A Walk?	Roy Fox ahb	Lon	21 Apr 31	Dec F-2318
Wrap Your Troubles In Dreams	Deauville Dance Band	Lon	– – Sep 31	EBR 1550
Writing A Letter To You	Roy Fox ahb	Lon	28 Jan 31	Dec F-2249
Ya Got Love	Roy Fox ahb	Lon	21 Apr 31	Dec F-2329
Ya Got Love	Jack Leon ahb	Lon	– – Jun 31	Pic 783
Yes! We Have No Bananas	New Mayfair Orc	Lon	14 Jul 31	HMV B-4012
Yes, Yes (My Baby Said Yes, Yes)	Roy Fox ahb	Lon	16 Oct 31	Dec F-2609
Yes, Yes (My Baby Said Yes, Yes)	Roy Fox ahb	Lon	2 Dec 31	Dec F-2720
You And The Night And The Music	AB acc orc dir Ray Noble	NY	12 Jan 35	Vic 24855
You Are My Heart's Delight	Roy Fox ahb	Lon	18 Aug 31	Dec F-2469*
You Brought A New Kind Of Love To Me	Alfredo ahb (duet LA)	Lon	17 Oct 30	EBW 5188
You Call It Madness	Roy Fox ahb	Lon	16 Oct 31	Dec rejected
You Call It Madness	Roy Fox ahb	Lon	2 Dec 31	Dec F-2720
You Call It Madness	New Cumberland Dance Orc	Lon	– – Jan 32	Film 379
You Can't Stop Me From Loving You	Roy Fox ahb	Lon	3 Sep 31	Dec F-2487
You Couldn't Be Cuter	Lew Stone ahb	Lon	12 Aug 38	Dec F-6745*
You Didn't Have To Tell Me	Roy Fox ahb	Lon	15 Apr 31	Dec F-2318
You Didn't Know The Music	Roy Fox ahb	Lon	7 Jan 32	Dec rejected
You Didn't Know The Music	AB acc Harry Hudson (p)	Lon	13 Jan 32	EBW 5470
You Didn't Know The Music	Roy Fox ahb	Lon	21 Jan 32	Dec F-2775

Title	Artiste	Place	Date	Original Issue
You Forgot Your Gloves	Roy Fox ahb	Lon	7 Oct 31	Dec F-2582
You Have Taken My Heart	Ray Noble aho	Lon	5 Apr 34	HMV B-6477
You, Just You	Ray Noble and the NMDO	Lon	11 Oct 32	HMV B-6251
You'll Always Be The Same Sweetheart To Me	Lew Stone and the Mons Band	Lon	2 Dec 32	Dec F-3345*
You'll Never Understand	Eddie Pola and Company 'America Calling'	Lon	25 Jul 33	Col DX-499
You Must Believe Me	AB	Lon	20 Apr 33	Dec F-3547
Younger Generation, The	Ray Noble and the NMDO	Lon	1 Sep 32	HMV B-6238, Vic 25020
You Opened My Eyes	AB acc orc dir Ray Noble	NY	15 Mar 35	HMV B-8330, BD-228, Vic 25004
You Ought To Be In Pictures	Ray Noble aho	Lon	5 Apr 34	HMV B-6477
You Ought To Be In Pictures	AB acc Monia Liter (p)	Lon	9 Apr 34	Dec F-3956
You Ought To See Sally On Sunday	Ray Noble aho	Lon	20 Dec 33	HMV B-6440, Vic 24575
You're As Pretty As A Picture	Geraldo aho	Lon	16 Dec 38	HMV BD-5444*
You're A Sweetheart	AB acc orc dir Ronnie Munro	Lon	2 Feb 38	HMV BD-503
You're A Sweetheart	Lew Stone ahb	Lon	4 Feb 38	Dec F-6606*
You're A Sweet Little Headache	Geraldo aho	Lon	3 Feb 39	HMV BD-5458*
You're Driving Me Crazy	Harry Hudson's Melody Men (duet LA)	Lon	9 Jan 31	EBR 1458
You're Driving Me Crazy	Novelty Orc	Lon	19 Feb 31	HMV B-3775, Vic 22745
You're Lucky To Me	Roy Fox ahb	Lon	5 Jan 31	Dec F-2194
You're Mine, You	Ray Noble aho	Lon	16 Jun 33	HMV B-6370
You're More Than All The World To Me	Ray Noble and the NMDO	Lon	1 Sep 32	HMV B-6237
You're My Everything	Roy Fox ahb	Lon	8 Aug 32	Dec F-3099
You're My Thrill	Lew Stone ahb	Lon	24 Apr 34	Dec F-3980*
You're The Kind Of Baby For Me	Savoy Hotel Orpheans	Lon	21 Jan 32	Col CB-403

Title	Artiste	Place	Date	Original Issue
You're The One I Care For	Roy Fox ahb	Lon	26 Feb 31	Dec F-2256
You're Twice As Nice As The Girl In My Dreams	NMDO	Lon	28 Apr 31	HMV B-6011
Yours Truly Is Truly Yours	Ray Noble aho	NY	19 Mar 36	Vic 25277*
You've Got What Gets Me	Roy Fox ahb	Lon	19 May 32	Dec F-3014
You Were There	Ray Noble aho	NY	7 Dec 36	Lon HMG-5027+ RT

Re-issues on Microgroove

Ever since microgroove records were introduced, recordings of Al Bowlly's have been re-issued on the new medium as either EPs (Extended Play) or LPs (Long Play). Many of these have now been deleted.

Since the main purpose of this section is to advise readers about albums currently available, only records still in the catalogue and therefore still obtainable are included. It is inevitable that since compiling this section some items will have been deleted. On the positive side, it is certain that further releases will have become available since going to press. In order to keep up-to-date with new releases of Al Bowlly (and all British nostalgia), readers are strongly advised to refer to *Memory Lane* magazine where all such records are reviewed.

Apart from all current albums devoted entirely to Al Bowlly, we have included records devoted either to a band or to various artistes where Bowlly is featured either on a considerable number of tracks or where a few Bowlly items are included that are considered to be of particular interest. This may be because the tracks are very rare, or not previously issued.

All the albums are of UK origin unless otherwise shown. In which ever country you live, the records listed, if still available, can be supplied by mail order from the specialist dealers advertising in *Memory Lane* magazine.

Where Al made more than one version of a title additional brief details have been included in brackets to enable it to be identified. Full details of all titles are to be found in the discography.

The Al Bowlly Circle. *Al Bowlly* President Joy 'D' 281
Cuddle Up Close; You'll Never Understand; Torn Sails; Moon; Gone For Ever; If You Were Only Mine; Call It A Day; Sweeping The Clouds Away; Who'll Buy An Old Gold Ring; Foolish Facts (AB); *Eleven More Months And Ten More Days* (AB); *Minnie The Moocher's Wedding Day; Roy Fox's Commentary On Minnie The Moocher's Wedding; Lazy Lou'siana Moon; Moonlight On The Colorado; Dark Clouds; Save The Last Dance For Me* (Savoy Hotel Orpheans).

Coffee In The Morning. *Lew Stone And His Band* President Lucky Evergreen Ple 505

Coffee In The Morning; Riptide; Looking For A Little Bit Of Blue; Because It's Love; Rolling Home; What A Little Moonlight Can Do; Love In Bloom; Wagon Wheels; With My Eyes Wide Open I'm Dreaming; Mauna Loa.

The Dance Band Days. *Al Bowlly* Decca RFLD 46 (Double Album)
Time On My Hands (Waldorfians); *I Can't Get Mississippi Off My Mind; Tell Me You Love Me; Moon; Linda* (Savoy Hotel Orpheans); *I'm Glad I Waited* (NMDO); *Heartaches; Goodnight Sweetheart* (Leon); *The Waltz You Saved For Me; Life Is Meant For Love; We've Got The Moon And Sixpence* (Noble); *The Longer That You Linger In Virginia; Springtime Reminds Me Of You; Roll On, Mississippi, Roll On* (Phillips); *Lady Play Your Mandoline; Time Alone Will Tell* (Phillips); *Can't We Be Friends; The Girl In The Upstairs Flat; Trusting My Luck; I'm Saving The Last Waltz For You; Somebody's Thinking Of You Tonight; Louisiana Hayride; It's A Long, Long Way To Your Heart; There's A Gold Mine In The Sky; Proud Of You; Souvenir Of Love; The Waves Of The Ocean Are Whispering Goodnight; Little Lady Make Believe* (Stone); *Fare Thee Well; Sweet Genevieve; Because It's Love; In My Little Red Book* (Stone); *In A Shelter From A Shower; I Won't Tell A Soul; Riding On A Haycart Home; Say Goodnight To Your Old Fashioned Mother.*

The Dance Band Years – The 1930s. *Various Artistes* Saville SVL 168
Change Partners; Shoe Shine Boy; Pennies From Heaven.

Dancing In The Dark. *Carroll Gibbons And The Savoy Hotel Orpheans* Saville SVL 157
Sweet And Lovely; Actions Speak Louder Than Words; I Heard; Try To Forget; She Didn't Say Yes; A Great Big Bunch Of You; Snuggled On Your Shoulder; What A Life; Goopy Geer; With All My Heart.

Dance Music Of The 1930s. *Roy Fox And His Band Featuring Al Bowlly* President Joy 'D' 266
Ya Got Love; Betty Co-Ed; Maybe It's Love; I'd Rather Be A Beggar With You; That Lindy Hop; One More Time; Smile, Darn You, Smile; Thank Your Father; You Forgot Your Gloves; Roll On Mississippi, Roll On; Bathing In The Sunshine; Between The Devil And The Deep Blue Sea; My Temptation; Sing Another Chorus, Please.

Dance Music Of The 1930s. *Roy Fox And His Band Vol 2* President Joy 'D' 275
Love You Funny Thing; Time Alone Will Tell; When The Waltz Was Through; Guilty; Goodnight Vienna; Living In Clover; The Echo Of A Song; Put That Sun Back In The Sky.

Dance Music Of The 1930s. *Carroll Gibbons 'Body And Soul'* President Joy 'D' 268
Who Am I?; Sweet And Lovely; There's A Time And Place For Everything; Linda.

Get Happy. *Lew Stone And His Band* Decca RFL 7
Weep No More, My Baby; Lonely Feet; Little Drummer Boy; In Santa Lucia; Who'll Buy An Old Gold Ring.

The Golden Age Of Al Bowlly *Al Bowlly* EMI GX 2512
Love Is The Sweetest Thing (Noble); *Bei Mir Bist Du Schoen* (AB); *Marie; In My Little Red Book* (Mantovani); *Something To Sing About; Walkin' Thru' Mockin' Bird Lane; My Melancholy Baby* (Liter); *Blow, Blow Thou Winter Wind; It Was A Lover And His Lass; Have You Ever Been Lonely; You're A Sweetheart* (AB); *Only Forever; Goodnight Sweetheart* (NMDO).

Goodnight Sweetheart Al Bowlly *(all with Ray Noble And His Orchestra)* EMI SH502
I'm Telling The World She's Mine; Goodnight Sweetheart; Lazy Day; Hang Out The Stars In Indiana; There's A Ring Around The Moon; Goodnight Vienna; I'll Do My Best To Make You Happy; Love Is The Sweetest Thing; Wanderer; Maybe I Love You Too Much; Shadow Waltz; I've Got To Sing A Torch Song; Close Your Eyes; Unless; Who Walks In When I Walk Out; Very Thought Of You, The; I'll String Along With You; Grinzing; Dreaming A Dream; Sing As We Go.

Goodnight Sweetheart – Al Bowlly 1931 Sessions. *Al Bowlly* Saville SVL 150
Time On My Hands (Godfrey); *What Are You Thinking About Baby?; Guilty* (Fox); *Take It From Me; Oh! Rosalita; Time Alone Will Tell* (Fox); *Thank Your Father; Would You Like To Take A Walk; I'll Keep You In My Heart Always; That's What I Like About You* (Godfrey); *Bubbling Over With Love* (Leon); *Just One More Chance; Dance Hall Doll; By The River Saint Marie* (Fox); *You Didn't Have To Tell Me; By My Side; Song Of Happiness; Lady Play Your Mandoline; Smile, Darn You, Smile; Goodnight Sweetheart* (Leon).

Great Bands In Digital Stereo Vol III. *Ray Noble And His Orchestra With Al Bowlly And Glenn Miller* RCA VPL1 0465
A Little White Gardenia; Top Hat; The Piccolino; You Opened My Eyes; St Louis Blues; Where The Lazy River Goes By; There's Something In The Air; Red Sails In The Sunset; Everything's Been Done Before; Big Chief De Sota; You And The Night And The Music.
Australian Issue

182

Great Singers Of The 1930s — Live Broadcasts. *Various Artistes*
Fanfare LP-40-140
It Was So Beautiful (Liter).
(Incorrectly titled and dated on the record sleeve).
US Issue

Heart And Soul. *Geraldo And His Orchestra With Al Bowlly* EMI EG
2604621/4
*My Heart Is Taking Lessons; On The Sentimental Side; In A Little Toy
Sailboat; Small Fry; Never Break A Promise; When Mother Nature Sings
Her Lullaby; Penny Serenade; Heart And Soul; Two Sleepy People; Is That
The Way To Treat A Sweetheart; Colorado Sunset; While A Cigarette Was
Burning; Any Broken Hearts To Mend; Summer's End; My Own; You're As
Pretty As A Picture; They Say; If Ever A Heart Was In The Right Place; One
Day When We Were Young; I'm In Love With Vienna.*

Heart And Soul. *Geraldo And His Orchestra 1938–41* Saville SVL 153
*Two Sleepy People; The Same Old Story; I Miss You In The Morning; My
Heart Is Taking Lessons; Heart And Soul; Deep In A Dream; Thanks For
Everything; Could Be; Between A Kiss And A Sigh.*

Hits Of The 1930s Vol 3. *Various Artistes* Decca RFLD 45 (Double
Album)
*Once In A While; Somebody's Thinking Of You Tonight; When The Organ
Played 'Oh Promise Me'* (Winnick).

The London Sessions 1928–30. *Al Bowlly* Saville SVL 148
Just Imagine; Wherever You Are (Elizalde); *If I Had You; Misery Farm; I'm
Sorry, Sally; When The Lilac Blooms Again; Up In The Clouds; After The
Sun Kissed The World Goodbye; If Anything Happened To You* (Elizalde);
*Happy Days Are Here Again; On The Sunny Side Of The Street; Sweeping
The Clouds Away; Dancing With Tears In My Eyes; Adeline; Beware Of
Love; Frankie And Johnnie; By The Old Oak Tree; Never Swat A Fly*
(Winter); *Sunny Days* (Winter); *Roamin Thru' The Roses.*

A Million Dreams. *Al Bowlly — Solos 1932–33* Saville SVL 163
*Wherever You Are; My Romance; I'll Do My Best To Make You Happy; Keep
Your Last Goodnight For Me; A Million Dreams; So Ashamed; I'll Follow
You; Glorious Devon; That's All That Matters To Me; Goodnight But Not
Goodbye; Maria My Own* (1933); *You Must Believe Me; There's A Cabin In
The Pines; Moonstruck; Learn To Croon; I'm Getting Sentimental Over You;
Love Locked Out; Night And Day; Fancy Our Meeting; Lover, Come Back To
Me.*

The One And Only Al. *Al Bowlly* Decca RFL 1
I've Had My Moments; I'm So Used To You Now (AB); *I'm For You A Hundred Per Cent; Whispering* (McDermott); *Dark Clouds; You Didn't Know The Music* (AB); *When We're Alone* (Fox); *It Was So Beautiful* (AB); *Ending With A Kiss; Melody In Spring; A Faded Summer Love; Tell Me, Are You From Georgia?; Beat O' My Heart* (Stone); *What A Perfect Night For Love* (Winter); *Rosa Mia; You Are My Heart's Delight; Dinah* (McDermott); *Leave The Rest To Nature* (AB).

Right From The Heart. *Lew Stone And His Band Featuring Al Bowlly* Old Bean Records OLD3
Rain Rain Go Away; Why Waste Your Tears; I Can't Write The Words; Someone To Care For; Three Wishes; I Lay Me Down To Sleep; In The Park In Paree; The Language Of Love; Isn't It Heavenly; Don't Change; The Day You Came Along; Thanks; Eadie Was A Lady; Gosh, I Must Be Falling In Love; What Is There To Take Its Place; I Love You Truly; As Long As I Live; Straight From The Shoulder.

Sentimentally Yours. *Al Bowlly* Conifer CHD127
Madonna Mine; I'm Getting Sentimental Over You; Judy; Everything I Have Is Yours; Glorious Devon; Isle Of Capri (AB); *Lover Come Back To Me* (1933 version); *There's A Cabin In The Pines* (AB); *If I Had A Million Dollars; True; It's All Forgotten Now* (AB); *The Very Thought Of You* (AB); *That's Me Without You; Fancy Our Meeting; Learn To Croon; Night And Day; Love Locked Out* (AB); *Be Still My Heart.*

Something To Sing About. *Al Bowlly With Geraldo And His Orchestra* EMI EG 2607851/4
Vieni, Vieni; Le Touquet; Smile When You Say Goodbye; Hometown; Something To Sing About; In My Little Red Book (Mantovani); *Grandma Said; Deep In A Dream; You're A Sweet Little Headache; I'm Madly In Love With You; The Same Old Story; Could Be; Between A Kiss And A Sigh; To Mother With Love; Thanks For Everything; I Miss You In The Morning; Small Town; What Do You Know About Love* (Williams); *Moon Love; Au Revoir But Not Goodbye.*
NB Not all the tracks on this record feature Geraldo and his Orchestra.

Sweet As A Song. *Al Bowlly (all solo recordings)* EMI EG 2604571/4
Carelessly; On A Little Dream Ranch; Blue Hawaii; Sweet Is The Word For You; Bei Mir Bist Du Schoen; Marie; You're A Sweetheart; The Pretty Little Patchwork Quilt; Sweet As A Song; Sweet Someone; Goodnight Angel; When The Organ Played 'O Promise Me'; Romany; Lonely; I Miss You In The Morning; A Violin In Vienna; What Do You Know About Love?; Hey Gypsy, Play Gypsy; South Of The Border; Dark Eyes.

Twenty Golden Greats. *Al Bowlly* EMI Records Australia SCA 060
*Love Is The Sweetest Thing; Time On My Hands; The Very Thought Of You;
You're Driving Me Crazy, Looking On The Bright Side Of Life; Please; A
Little Street Where Old Friends Meet; Have You Ever Been Lonely; The
Moment I Saw You; The Old Spinning Wheel; Thanks; My Song Goes Round
The World; Did You Ever See A Dream Walking; Goodnight Sweetheart; I
Love You Truly; All I Do Is Dream Of You;* (All foregoing titles with
Noble/NMDO.) *Sweet And Lovely* (Savoy Hotel Orpheans); *It's A Lovely Day
Tomorrow; Dark Eyes; Over The Rainbow.*
Australian Issue

We Danced All Night. *Ray Noble And His Orchestra Featuring Al Bowlly*
RCA International NL 89463
Easy To Love (Sep 36); *Why Stars Come Out At Night; Soon; The Touch Of
Your Lips* (Mar 36); *I've Got You Under My Skin.*

We'll Be Together Again. *Al Bowlly And The Masqueraders* Limited
Edition Records LE5001
*Actions Speak Louder Than Words; One Little Quarrel; Granny's Photo
Album; Kiss By Kiss; The Night You Gave Me Back The Ring; Only Me
Knows Why; With Love In My Heart; Take Away The Moon; We'll Be
Together Again; Tell Tales; Try To Forget; She Didn't Say Yes; The King
Was In The Counting House; Goopy Geer; Sailing On The Robert E. Lee;
Listen To The German Band.*
Australian Issue

Filmography

Al Bowlly made only a few film appearances. On several, he is seen as a member of a dance band but is not heard vocally. Some of these arose because Lew Stone, of whose band Al was a member, was Musical Director for British and Dominion Films. On a couple he is not seen but heard singing over the 'credits'. Some of these films made over 50 years ago by companies which no longer exist have probably not survived. Indeed there are seven I have not been able to view. These are included because there is documentary evidence indicating a strong possibility that Al is seen and/or heard singing in them.

There have been several post-war films in which a photograph of Al Bowlly is seen or his voice from a gramophone record is heard. Such films are not included in the listing which follows.

Title And Company Unknown 1930
This is a 'short' of the Blue Boys of which Al Bowlly was a member. He is likely to be seen and may also be heard vocally.

It Ain't No Fault Of Mine* PATHÉ 1932
This is a short of Roy Fox and his Band. Nat Gonella takes the vocal but Al Bowlly is seen in the band playing guitar. He is not heard vocally.

A Night Like This BRITISH AND DOMINION 1932
Al Bowlly is seen with a band directed by Lew Stone singing through a megaphone 'In London On A Night Like This'.

Antoinette BRITISH AND DOMINION 1932
Al Bowlly is not seen, but is thought to be heard singing the title song.

Love Contract, The BRITISH AND DOMINION 1932
Al Bowlly may be seen or heard as it is thought that Lew Stone and his Band made an appearance.

New Empire Review Presents Roy Fox And His Band And Douglas Byng NEW EMPIRE REVIEW 1932
Al Bowlly is seen as a member of Roy Fox's Band playing guitar. He is not heard vocally.

Bitter Sweet BRITISH AND DOMINION 1933
Al Bowlly is seen playing guitar as a member of a dance band consisting

of Lew Stone's musicians playing 'I'll See You Again'. He is not heard vocally.

Just My Luck BRITISH AND DOMINION 1933

Al Bowlly may be seen or heard as it is thought that Lew Stone and his Band made an appearance.

Little Damozel, The BRITISH AND DOMINION 1933

It is thought that Al Bowlly is heard singing over the 'credits' the song 'What More Can I Ask?'.

Little Nell SILENT HOME MOVIE PROBABLY 1933

Al Bowlly can be seen enacting 'Little Nell' with Lew Stone and his Band.

Mayor's Nest, The BRITISH AND DOMINION 1933

Al Bowlly has a small acting part. He is seen singing 'The Wedding Of The Slumtown Babies' and 'Say To Yourself "I Will Be Happy"'.

Up For The Derby BRITISH AND DOMINION 1933

Al Bowlly may be seen or heard as it is thought that Lew Stone and his Band made an appearance.

Now Pathétone Has Pleasure In Presenting Al Bowlly PATHÉTONE WEEKLY 1934

Al Bowlly performs his then recent record release 'The Very Thought Of You' accompanied by Monia Liter (piano).

My Melancholy Baby* PATHÉ PICTORIAL 1936

Al Bowlly performs his then recent record release 'My Melancholy Baby' accompanied by Monia Liter (piano).

*The copies of these films viewed have no title as such, as was probably the case originally. The title shown in the Filmography is of the song performed.

Index

The index which follows contains an entry for all the names mentioned in the main text. Where the page number is set in italics, the entry refers to an illustration.

Where specific artistes whose names are mentioned in the main text also recorded with Al Bowlly, the relevant page number of the discography is also shown against the entry in the index. However this cross-referencing has not been included with bands such as those led by Ray Noble or Roy Fox with whom Bowlly made numerous recordings because these appear on the majority of pages of the discography.